LANGUAGE POLICY IN THE PRIMARY SCHOOL:
Content and Management

Language Policy in the Primary School:

Content and Management

ERIC ASHWORTH

CROOM HELM
London • New York • Sydney

129622

© 1988 Eric Ashworth
Croom Helm Ltd, Provident House,
Burrell Row, Beckenham, Kent BR3 1AT

Croom Helm Australia, 44-50 Waterloo Road,
North Ryde, 2113, New South Wales

Published in the USA by
Croom Helm
in association with Methuen, Inc.
29 West 35th Street
New York, NY 10001

British Library Cataloguing in Publication Data

Ashworth, Eric
  Language policy in the primary school:
  content and management.
  1. Language arts (Elementary) — Great
  Britain
  I. Title
  372.6'0941   LB1576

  ISBN 0-7099-5128-0
  ISBN 0-7099-5140-X Pbk

Library of Congress Cataloging-in-Publication Data

Ashworth, Eric.
  Language policy in the primary school.

  1. Language arts (Elementary) — Great Britain.
2. English language — Study and teaching (Elementary) —
Great Britain. 3. Children — Great Britain — Language.
I. Title.
LB1576.A716 1988   372.6'0941   87-30334
ISBN 0-7099-5128-0
ISBN 0-7099-5140-X (pbk.)

Printed and bound in Great Britain by Mackays of Chatham Ltd, Kent

Contents

Contents

1

Why Each Primary School Should Have a Language Policy

The Bullock Committee's report *A Language for Life* is the most useful survey of language teaching and of the place of language in learning that has yet come from official sources in Britain. Among the most important of the Committee's recommendations was one to the effect that each school should develop for itself its own language policy. Since then there have been many courses, more meetings and much activity but, in my view at least, not much real progress. Though there are all sorts of reasons for this, none of them has to do with any lessening of the need for a language policy. The failure to make greater advances has been the result of certain factors, many of which have to do with a shortage of knowledge and professional expertise among teachers and heads and which has been most pronounced in two areas: knowledge of what language is and how it can be taught and learned; and in the skills of applying appropriate management techniques.

Teachers need knowledge of various kinds and they also need to acquire a range of related skills if they are to be able first to formulate and then to implement a language policy. This book tries to identify this knowledge and these skills and makes suggestions which, it is hoped, may prove to be useful to teachers and heads. This chapter looks again, as the Bullock Committee did, at the need for a language policy on which the need for such knowledge and skills depends. First, it considers some of the reasons why language is itself so important, and then it goes on to ask whether this importance means that there should therefore be a language policy in every school. It will ask, that is, why we cannot just let language be and why we cannot carry on in the old pre-Bullock ways. Then, it will pause briefly to consider what, in any case, a language policy is or should be.

1

The importance of language

Much of what can be said about the importance of language seems to be self-evident. Speaking and listening, reading and writing, are clearly vital both in expressing oneself and in communicating with others. And much of the developmental importance of language comes about because of this.

It is largely because of its potential in communication that language plays its part in the social and emotional development of children. The child who has no language, or whose language is grossly inadequate for the normal uses of his age, is likely thereby to be impaired socially and emotionally as well. The child who cannot talk to others misses companionship and the opportunity to make those close ties which pave the way for normal development. Further, if he cannot 'talk' to himself he lacks a safety valve, for language can take the place of less desirable outlets such as violence and tantrums. He is also without a principal means of coming to terms with life and its joys and troubles, of reflecting on happenings, of teasing out the complexities of all sorts of human and non-human relationships, and of using language to comfort himself. Examples of the effects of such gross language impairment can be seen in the careers of children born profoundly deaf who, compared with hearing children, are likely to be more emotionally immature and unstable.

Language is important in other ways. Some of these will be examined in Chapter 7 on language in learning and across the curriculum. Here, we need to note that it performs an essential function in allowing a child to draw the attention of others and to fix his own — which is the essential basis both for much human interaction and for a great proportion of his own cognitive functioning. It provides a means for representing and classifying events, actions and experiences and thus for dealing with them and bringing the world to order. It goes much further in this respect than merely providing names for classes; it enables such classes (and this includes classes of persons, of events and of actions) to be related to each other in various ways that are meaningful. In short, language allows thinking and reasoning to be extended far beyond what would be possible without it. At the same time, through that communicative power which was mentioned earlier, it gives access to the thinking of others from times past and places distant as well as from the here and now. Of course, other means of development are open to individuals who lack language. Some sorts of thinking and classifying are certainly possible without language. What language does for those who are competent in its use is to facilitate and advance, to make easier what might be immensely difficult or tedious without it.

And it is true that whole ranges of thinking seem to be quite impossible without language. For example, understanding cause and effect relationships, except at the most primitive and obvious level, seems to require linguistic formulation. While there are other ways of representing phenomena to oneself, such as by images or by enactive traces, language is the most generalised, subtle, flexible and, probably, the most potent means of representing reality. And of course, because of its origins in human interactions, it is the means that lends itself most readily to the *communication* of such thinking. Its rivals in this respect — mathematical symbolisings, dance, painting, movement, the notations of formal logic — all have their important places, but in terms of their significance to the individual as well as to society none can stand comparison with language.

Also we live in a culture that is permeated by language and there are hardly any aspects of communal or individual life that are not in some way profoundly touched by it.

What is a language policy?

Shortly we shall go on to consider the case for having a language policy but before then it might be useful to indicate what is meant by that term. What follows is offered with the needs of primary schools of all kinds in mind, whose children range from those in the nursery years to the oldest juniors — from 3-11 years of age.

Within such a range there are, of course, considerable variations and parts of what is said will be more relevant to the earliers years and other parts to the later years. For example, nursery classes and nursery schools will not want to pay too much attention to the development of writing, though they would be wise to examine its developmental prerequisites and to cater for them. Much of what will be said about the development of study skills is geared more to the needs of middle and top juniors than to those of younger children. Nevertheless, it is an important principle of management that the staff as a whole should take responsibility for the policy as a whole, and so it is desirable that in the all-through primary school there should be no parochialism. It is both desirable and

3

profitable that the school which deals with only one part of the primary phase should take a developmental view and give regard to both the earlier and later stages of progression, understanding, so to speak, both where their children have come from and where they are going to. When this happens it is usually accompanied by great gains, in the staff, of professional confidence.

Be that as it may, in practical terms making a language policy centres on the production of a document which itself will come to be known as the school's language policy. That document itself will be of cardinal importance but the processes that lie behind it are just as important. Much more will be said about these in Chapter 8 dealing with management. Essentially, they involve discussion about the ways in which language, or any part of it, is learned and with what can be done to assist that learning. In order to help these processes, it might be helpful to think of them in terms of a three-phase cycle involving planning, implementing and evaluating — what might be called the PIE model. A language policy document will incorporate the results of planning, and it will also indicate the principal ways of implementing and evaluating what is done.

As a brief and tentative summary, then, we might say that we are thinking in terms of a document that deals with the learning and the use of the four skills of language — listening, speaking, reading and writing — throughout the primary years. This may sound extensive enough. In fact, it will lead us further — right into the curriculum as a whole and into the whole nexus of human relations in and around the school.

The educational reasons for a language policy

Given that language is important in the ways we outlined earlier, does this mean that there should inevitably be a language policy? If language is as all-pervasive and important as was made out, will it not simply look after itself? Is not language growth natural? Even if it is not spontaneous, cannot we rely on individual teachers to do separately all that is necessary to help their children? The answer to these questions is 'No!'

In the first place it would be very difficult for any single teacher to have the expertise necessary to help all her children. There can never be any question of splitting up language work into neat and discrete parcels each to be dealt with as a year's work, so that all any teacher would need would be to become expert only in that part of language work apportioned to her. In any sizeable group of children there will be considerabe ranges of ability and attainment. For instance, a teacher of infant children whose class was visited by the author showed the results of a reading test which indicated that there was a spread of over 6 years in their reading ages. Her children were mostly just turned 7 years of age, and as they grew older it was likely that the spread would increase rather than diminish. In so far as this is typical of other skills and of children in other schools, it would not make sense to think that there is either a single level of attainment or specific and narrow ranges of skills with which a class teacher can in real life be solely concerned. From this it follows that each school ought, at the very least, to coordinate all the overlapping work of its teachers so that all children, the quick and the slow, the advanced and the backward, the older and the younger, can find sensible and coherent pathways through. These pathways need to be arraged so that there is consistency and continuity in the treatment of each single child. Such planning clearly needs to be school-wide and not merely class-wide.

There are other reasons why schools should have a unified policy and they are just as compelling. The major skills of language are interdependent. Listening, speaking, reading and writing all affect, and are affected by, each other. With normal progress in the primary years, each nourishes and is nourished by the others. Some of the precise ways in which this happens will be considered in later chapters. It follows from this interdependence that no skill should be neglected by any teacher at any point in the school; otherwise, the whole of the language work will be in some danger. As a simple instance, spoken language needs to be developed throughout the whole of the primary years, not only for its own sake but because it assists in diverse ways the learning of reading and writing.

To summarise, the main educational reason for having a language policy is that it will provide some sort of assurance that all the language skills will be developed throughout the school and also that this development will be coordinated by teachers so that the growth of competence of all the children will become truly and maximally cumulative, with each skill contributing in some measure to the development of the others.

There is, however, more to it than this. There are several other educational considerations which serve to underline the need to formulate, operate, and review language work as a whole. The first is the obvious one that it presents the school with a major opportunity of reviewing and further developing its whole curriculum.

5

Because language is so far-reaching, there is at such a time a possibility of radical change. When we think not just of learning language but also of using language in other learning, this sense of a radical opportunity is enhanced. Making a language policy, then, brings the chance, if one should want to take it, of a major replanning of the work of the school.

Closely allied to this is the opportunity that the enterprise brings for staff development. Curriculum development, in whatever area, makes no sort of sense without corresponding staff development. The very process of discussing the problems associated with learning, teaching, and using language is itself likely to be a significant piece of staff development, if it is handled properly. As the process goes on, new needs are likely to be identified which, if met, will cause staff expertise to be raised to new heights. We shall consider these matters more fully when we deal with the role of the head in the management of a language policy.

The 'political' reasons for a language policy

Such managerial matters afford a convenient bridge between the more purely educational reasons for a language policy with which we dealt earlier and a set of 'political' reasons whose source is external to the school.

We mentioned earlier the three-phase model — the PIE model — of which the third phase was evaluation. This is the phase that it would be easy to ignore or diminish. But there are today very strong reasons for insisting that evaluating its work ought to be very much a part of a school's responsibilities and, consequently, that the techniques for doing so ought to become part of the teacher's professional competence. In other words, to the notion that the teacher's job is mainly in face-to-face encounters with children, we need to add the responsibilities for planning in depth and also for evaluating the whole business of teaching and learning.

The professional reason for this is that no individual (and no school) is likely to get all his language work right, or even optimal, at the first attempt. The idea of evaluating is the same as saying that teachers are willing to learn from experience and that they will do something to systematise the fruits of that experience in order to put their conclusions to good effect in improving their work with children. That itself is reason enough. Its 'political' aspects make the case even stronger.

One of the significant movements affecting education both in this country and in America in recent years is the call for accountability. At one level this is perfectly justifiable, for it is the public purse that pays for public education and it is a principle that public money cannot be disbursed without financial accountability. In practice, the problem becomes one of deciding how detailed that accountability should be and what forms it should take. No-one is against straightforward financial accounting. The difficulty is that 'accountability' can mean a whole range of possibilities. It can mean explaining — to parents, governors, the public, the children — what is being attempted and why. There is everything to be said for this sort of accountability. It is an excellent discipline for the profession. Communication about education has been, sadly, lacking in the past. But 'accountability' can also be part of a process whereby effective control passes to agencies external to the school. We can ask how far the control of decisions both about what is taught and about how it is taught should be located outside the school. The dividing line between control by central or local government and the autonomy of the school is, and has always been, a difficult one to draw. Where there is consensus, the problem, except as a matter of abstract principle, does not become urgent. But in some circumstances external control can take forms that lead to abuse and which are ultimately anti-educational.

Payment by results is an example of this. Long abandoned in the United Kingdom itself, it has reappeared in some American school systems where sometimes outside contractors are paid *if* they come in and get results. In the United Kingdom itself a voucher system has been advocated — which means that parents would subscribe only to the sort of schooling of which they approved — and a former Secretary of State for Education and Science himself declared his sympathy with the principle, though the practicalities defeated him. Under this system, if it became operative, consumer sovereignty would reach new heights; resources would be diverted to those schools which were 'good'; schools which thus delivered the goods would survive, others would perish. Ultimately, in such a system it would not be the teacher who decided what was to be taught or even how it was to be taught.

At the same time, governors of schools, including parent governors, have been given greater powers over school management and some of these impinge directly or indirectly on the curriculum. Local educational inspectorates have been increased in size. Both they and Her Majesty's Inspectorate make claims and give guidance about what the curriculum should be — guidance which is backed by both direct and indirect means of control. On top of this there is the monitoring of language work done by the Assessment of Performance Unit which was set up on the recommendation of the Bullock Committee. All these innovations have the effect of decreasing the powers of the schools to decide their own curricula. It is true to say that there is already great influence and power on the curriculum exercised from outside the school and that this tendency is growing.

The author's view is that there is great danger in these developments. There is a possibility that teachers will have foisted upon them a narrow view of their own proper responsibilities. It would be founded on the idea that their job is essentially that of day-to-day teaching centred upon face-to-face encounters with children, while both the wider aspects of the job and those considerations which really determine the scope of teaching in this narrower sense would be controlled and decided elsewhere. In the author's view, the development of the teaching profession ought to lie in an expansion, and not in a contraction, of its responsibilities. It ought to be possible to say something like this:

> Teachers will conduct dialogues with all manner of interested parties — with employers, with governors, with advisers and inspectors, with parents and, not least, with children — but at the end of the day the resolution of any conflicts and the making of decisions about the curriculum, within whatever global finance is allowed, are the responsibility of teachers, for one reason above others. If they do not have this responsibility, their professional development will be impaired; they will become less good at face-to-face teaching because the decisions which determine it, and which should lie within the professional sphere, are no longer theirs. As a result, they will come to rely on others; they will not need to understand in depth such matters as the structure of subjects on the one hand, or the needs of balanced curriculum planning on the other. In short, losing responsibility for the curriculum will be a diminishing and enervating process.

The consequences of such changes would be dire. Teachers, whether they realised it or not, would be reduced to something like the status of auxiliaries, on a par with the nursery nurses and infant helpers of the present day. Both the regard in which they are held by the public and the salary they are paid would surely drop. Yet it is clear, on the other hand, that authorities, governors, parents and others do have their own legitimate concerns. How are the interests of the two sides to be reconciled?

It needs to be established as a first principle that the concerns of non-teachers ought not to extend to the right to prescribe either curriculum or method. Nevertheless, they ought to have the right to see that a school is well-managed, not merely in the sense of being orderly and free from abuse, but in the sense that proper professional concern is being given to the curriculum, to the futherance of that extended professional competence to which it is linked and, perhaps most importantly, to be assured that a continuous process of review, reformulation and improvement is under way. It follows from this that the proper people to plan, review, and where necessary to reformulate the curriculum are the teachers themselves, working as members of school staffs. It is neither necessary nor desirable that they should do this in isolation. On the contrary, it is a process which affords great opportunities for learning from others both in and out of the school system. It pushes us towards the PIE model — which is why that model is advocated here. How it would work in practice is left to Chapter 8.

Note

For convenience I shall refer to the head and pupil as 'he' and to the teacher as 'she'.

2

Understanding What Language Is

Having established the main reasons why primary schools should develop their own language policies, and having related this to the good management of the school, we now turn the other focus of this book which is language itself. Here we face a curious problem, for we are already experts in language, and if we are experts can there be any point in pursuing the matter further? However, the problem is soon solved, for while we are indeed skilled in using language — at least for many purposes — we are not necessarily either clear or profound in our understanding of it and the way it works. Nor are we always secure in our ability to be articulate about it. What follows in this chapter, then, is offered in the conviction that teachers need to develop certain understandings and to become articulate about them before the work of planning policies can proceed. Ideas of the ways in which language can be taught and learned are founded upon such understandings; and the business of formulating a policy through discussion necessarily requires both understanding and the possession of a coherent set of ideas which can be expounded, tested, advanced, modified and further clarified through the teacher's own language.

Ways of looking at language — some basic matters of linguistics and psychology

There are different ways of looking at language and different sorts of understanding are possible. The same is true, of course, of many other phenomena as well as language. Think, for example, of a landscape. You and I might be concerned with the beauty of the scene. A geologist might be more concerned with the underlying strata and their outcroppings. A farmer might see opportunities for growing even more oilseed rape. One geographer might be concerned with plotting the land forms and other topographical features, while another, historically minded, might be more concerned with chronological dimensions as he plots changes in land-use and settlement patterns. Other geographers might be more interested in the distribution of the crops and of other vegetation. Painters might see changing patterns of light as they interplay with more stable, but still changing, features such as the rivers, the hills and the grasses. Poets might see all of these things and go on to transform them into a metaphor for the characteristics of humankind.

There are, similarly, quite different perspectives from which it is possible to look at language. A physicist, for example, might be interested in its acoustic properties, a singer in its production at the right pitch, with acceptable tone and at the right tempo. A neurologist, on the other hand, might be concerned with the neural structures that underlie speech production and with the ways in which they function. Psychologists are mainly interested in speech as a form of behaviour. Sociologists look at such matters as how speech is affected, for example, by social stratification. Linguists are interested in language as patterns of words, sounds and grammar.

From the teacher's point of view, it is unlikely that any single discipline will provide all that she needs; her understanding needs to be multidisciplinary, gathering insights from wherever they are to be found (while taking care that the 'insights' are truly compatible with each other). Accordingly, what follows in this chapter will draw indirectly on the work of many scholars from different fields, but mainly from linguistics and psychology. Within disciplines there are different schools of thought, each with different strengths and different weaknesses and so it may be advisable to tell the reader briefly where the author stands in relation to certain contentious matters in linguistics and psychology, for those are the disciplines on which we shall depend most of all.

One benefit which we may hope to gain from linguistics is some sort of clarification of what it is that children *actually* learn when they learn language. Unfortunately for us if we are seeking simple outcomes, linguists are deely divided. Perhaps the most vigorous and influential, particularly in America, is Noam Chomsky whose work has been seminal there. The brief discussion which follows can do no sort of justice to him as a thinker, as a linguist, or as a man whose generous concern for the human race informs all he does. However, it will serve the dual purposes of introducing some of the issues with which we shall have to deal as we pursue our understandings, and of making the author's own position clear in regard to them.

Chomsky founded his version of grammar on a distinction between the 'deep' and the 'surface' structures of language. By 'deep structures' he meant, very roughly, certain underlying features of a language which are not themselves amenable to the senses. They cannot be seen or heard. By 'surface structure', again very roughly, he meant those features of a language which are amenable to the senses — in a way they are the outcroppings of language. His estimation of what an ordinary speaker must acquire in order to be considered competent, coupled with an insistence that psychology was unable to account for this acquisition, led him to make the startling declaration that the deep aspects of language were not learned at all, but were acquired through the mechanisms of heredity. In other words, they were innate. Humans were born with language. It was there at birth already in the mind, in a 'skeletal' form, waiting to be fleshed out, through the actual manifestations of language in whatever particular community the child happened to be born.

The present writer's own analysis does not derive any support from Chomsky's ideas. Rather, it is founded on a view of language which does not make such fundamental distinctions as those which Chomsky drew between deep and surface structures and which has no need to postulate that language is in any sense innate. What does seem to be innate, though, is a capability for learning language — and for learning much else as well. There seems to be, contrary to what Chomsky thought, nothing so special about the acquisition of language that marks it off from other sorts of learning for which human beings also have a marked propensity. Language is not, in my view, to be absolutely differentiated from other sorts of behaviour and knowledge. Indeed, one of the major themes that we shall develop is that learning language actually depends on other sorts of learning which then become an indispensable part of the whole process of making and construing meanings through language.

Chomskyan theory is also about a set of rules which enables the possessor to generate an infinite number of correct sentences. Chomsky uses this idea to stress the infinite creativity of language. It involves us in a paradox, however, for insistence on this kind of generation obscures elements of choice which the competent human possesses — such as being silent (when no generative rules would apply). More importantly, it does not stress the ways in which language is always related to circumstances and to other human beings, to their understandings and, very often, to their own production of language.

Fortunately, there is another tradition within linguistics in the United Kingdom as well as in the United States. In this other tradition there is no exclusive concern with the rules which generate language. Instead, language is linked to the wider contexts and situations in which it occurs. Such Americans as Martin Joos and Dell Hymes have developed theories to explain these connections and Hymes's notion of communicative competence (which I greatly prefer in opposition to Chomsky's notion of generative competence) contains a great deal which we shall find useful. In Britain, relating language to situation is part of the current orthodoxy among linguists. Mainstream linguistics, as exemplified in the work of Firth, Malinowski and others, centres on models of language which, quite intrinsically and not as a mere afterthought, link language production and use to widening contexts and situations including such features as the audience, the physical surroundings, and even the wider aspects of culture. This conceptualisation is an important influence on everything that follows in this book.

The rejection of Chomsky's notion that a large part of language is innate and the acceptance of a linguistic model that stresses the importance of situation and context are two steps that take us outwards from linguistics and into other areas in search of further understanding. In order to explicate language, and then the learning of language, more fully, we shall find it necessary to go beyond linguistics and to draw upon psychology and sociology.

Before we can do this, it is again fitting to make clear the writer's own position. It is one of strong reaction against two streams of psychology which have co-mingled with, I think, dire results. Both, incidentally, are part of what Chomsky decided was inadequate to explain the individual's acquisition of language. In this he was right. But whereas his conclusion was to posit that therefore language must in some sense be innate, a more profitable outcome might have been to call for changes in psychology itself.

The first of the two streams is what is known as stimulus-response psychology. Historically, its basic assumptions seem to have been drawn from those which were supposed to pertain in natural science. You have a piece of metal, say, and you do something to it such as changing its temperature. You heat it and you measure what you do. You also measure the results of what you do. You then relate the two, having discounted or 'controlled for' other variables (for example, changes in atmospheric pressure) which might affect the results and you then draw conclusions about correlations and maybe also about cause-and-effect relationships from what you have done. We could note in passing that this is no longer a universally accepted paradigm even for natural science. The trouble with applying it to living creatures and especially to human beings is that exogenous changes (from without the organism) encounter all sorts of endogenous changes (those within the organism) which may then interact with each other. When notions such as consciousness and will are introduced, these interactions are no longer mechanistic and the physical model of natural science becomes irrelevant and misleading. Consequently, the efforts of those psychologists who use this paradigm, or minor variations of it, are doomed in advance. Words such as 'consciousness', 'intention', 'purpose', and so on give us a valuable hint about its inadequacy. Any model which looks upon human beings as being the legitimate objects of stimulus-response activities and which thus ignores human individuality is, I believe, degrading as well as ultimately unproductive.

The other stream in psychology to which I find myself opposed is behaviourism. This began as a commendable seeking after scientific rigour. Ideas such as consciousness, purpose, intention, and mind itself were, and are, difficult to deal with. Behaviourist psychologists do not so much deny the existence of such phenomena as disown them. They say, in effect, 'The proper concern of psychology as a rigorous science is with what can be observed either through the senses directly or through some extension of them such as the microscope.' This concern for the observable became tied up with a concern for measuring what they observed and this latter was a most unhealthy development. In various appearances it has buttressed some notions, which seem distinctly odd to me — for example, that intelligence is measurable, that it is fixed enough to be measurable and, by extension, to the notion that it is predetermined. Thus behaviourism has served to reinforce other tendencies in psychology, even some of those which to begin with had quite different histories and divergent concerns from those of behaviourism itself.

The most distinctive concern of behaviourism, that of limiting the scope of psychology as a science, has had unfortunate results. Within the limits that it imposes it is not possible to account for, for instance, how human beings form intentions which then influence their subsequent behaviour. Expectations are another concept with which behaviourists cannot really cope. Yet it seems clear that once expectations are formed, they direct attention, help to form learning sets (or inclinations to learn), shape the selection of possible inputs to the expecting organism and provide, as it were, working hypotheses by which significance and meaning are to be reached and understood. One can see that once expectations, purposes, intentions and the like are admitted to the scene, the old paradigm is broken. In other words, beings that can exercise such attributes can no longer be considered as the passive recipients of experimental changes. Indeed, even to subject them to many of the experiments which psychologists have tried in the past is, in my view, to insult them.

All this is highly contentious. But there seems to be no doubt that learning language is in part learning to form intentions and to use certain purposes as guides which shape that language. And it seems clear that the efficient comprehension of both speech and writing cannot be accounted for until we take expectations (of meaning) into our reckoning. Unless such concepts are admitted, there is, it seems, no possibility of explaining the ease and despatch with which most individuals acquire the skills of language.

Such are the assumptions and prejudices which underlie what follows. They inform the view of language, language learning and, of course, language use, that is propounded in this and in later chapters. Probably my position is not too far from that which most teachers already hold. Right or wrong, they seek to enhance rather than diminish the notion of what human beings as language-users are like and thus of what it is to be human. In this book, then, humans are actors who shape their own behaviour and thus their learning; they are not merely things to be acted upon.

What is language?

Before we can show how these ideas work out in practice, we need to try to refine our notion of what language is. In the first place it is a means of recording, expressing, or communicating meaning. Now, there are several systems that are sometimes loosely or metaphorically called 'language'. There is the 'language' of music, of movement, of art, and of dance. Then there is what has come to be known as 'body language'. There is no denying that all these phenomena are important and one can understand why people might want to refer to them as languages. Nevertheless, one would wish to deny the use of the term 'language' to refer to them. It is true that all of them express and communicate and some of them also record. They share other attributes with language itself in that they are usually systematic, with their parts being internally related to one another. But the essence of anything properly to be called language in this book is that it should possess both words and grammar systematically related to each other.

Thus we are working with a somewhat restricted idea of language. Yet it is still very extensive. We can talk of the French language and of the English language as examples. And we can talk of the dialects which are related to those and other languages, such as Cockney or Lancashire which are regional in location. There are also class dialects. Standard English is itself partly regional (in origin) and partly class, originating in the south Midlands and becoming the accepted dialect of the court and eventually of the educated classes.

Dialects and accents

Dialects share the general attributes of all languages. What is significant about them is that they are languages of particular communities or classes. In many regions of the United Kingdom dialects exist and are used side by side with other dialects. Linguists who have mapped their locations find variations from valley to valley and sometimes from street to street. It then becomes a matter of the way in which we define dialects before we can say how many there are. One can map subtle changes right across Lancashire and Yorkshire so that it is doubtful whether we can speak of *the* Yorkshire dialect or *the* Lancashire dialect unless we use those terms to signify a generic collection of similar but not identical languages. Internally, as systems, dialects share certain attributes with all other spoken languages. They have words, they have sound patterns and they have grammar. Whether one language is better than another, or whether one dialect is better than another dialect, is a difficult question to answer. Linguists, on the whole, are reluctant even to consider the matter. As a system, one language may be pretty much like another. Aesthetically, some languages may be rated higher than others, largely one suspects because beauty is in the ear of the listener rather than in any qualities intrinsic to the language

16

itself. It is also true that some languages and dialects are put to distinctive uses, in contrast to others which may be put to different uses. The scholarly and liturgical uses of Arabic and Latin are examples of this. The distinction matters to teachers, because regional dialects tend to be frowned upon in speech and are regarded as anathema in writing. So rigid has this become that all dialects except standard English are radically excluded from the examination system. Children who wish to pass public examinations had better try to do it in standard English, whatever their 'mother' dialect.

Accent is a different matter. It is made up of distinctive ways of pronouncing language and it, too, has a regional or social base. Regional accents are now tolerated in ways that hardly seemed possible 40 years ago. It is, in theory, possible to use any accent with any dialect. In practice, we do not find a regional dialect, such as one from Lancashire, being spoken in, say, a London accent, though sensitive ears may detect its influences. What we do often find, however, is standard English being spoken with a regional accent.

Different listeners have their own preferences for accents. Most of us regard our own accent as 'normal' and have degrees of liking and disliking other people's. If there is a difficulty with a 'broad' accent, it is not that it is intrinsically inferior to other accents, but that it may turn out to be unintelligible to other listeners. A 'broad' accent in that case is only one which is very different from the accent of the surrounding community. Nevertheless, as with dialect, there may be matters of prestige involved. There seems to be a sort of bargain between some private schools and the parents of their children that they will inculcate that accent known as Received Pronunciation — which is something like that used by BBC newsreaders, presenters of Radio Three and, perhaps, Sloane Rangers. Such an accent does, unfortunately in my view, have a large measure of social prestige which may be valuable in deciding who shall be given a job and who shall join, or be excluded from, a social group. But that this should be so says more about the nature of a class-conscious society than it does about the quality or the intrinsic usefulness of the accent.

The two modes of language — written and spoken

It was noted above that language, at least within the limits we have put to it, is made up of several components. Before we examine them further we must point to the fact that most, but not all, languages have two modes — the spoken and the written. A great deal of what follows in this book depends on an understanding of these modes and of the similarities and differences between them. For the moment it is enough to note that the written mode is not simply the spoken mode written down. It is true that the two modes have much in common. That is why both could be called 'English'. Each has its own word stock, or lexicon, but the majority of words can be used in both. However, each mode also has a rich life of its own, and it is the differences between the two that must be successfully negotiated if the learner is to become proficient in both. As we shall see, it is impossible for a speaker to become literate unless he understands a good deal about how the written mode differs from the spoken.

The most obvious component of the spoken mode is its sounds. Of course, if it is to qualify as language it will also have words and grammar and these may differ from those found in writing, but it is the sounds component that distinguishes it most clearly from the written mode. Within the sounds component two elements are important for our purposes. The first is those basic constituent sounds of the language which are called *phonemes*. There are over 40 of them in English, though the number varies slightly with the regional accent. While they are the basic sounds of English, they are not in fact produced quite identically by all users of the language. This is partly because of anatomical and physiological differences between people — the young from the old, men from women, and so on, but accent may also be involved.

In addition to these basic constituent sounds there are the larger sounds which are sometimes called intonation patterns. Phonemes are combined to make words. Words, either singly or in strings, are uttered with some sort of tune. That tune is the intonation pattern. Its purpose is to convey signals which the listener will take as meaningful. For example, there are distinctive tunes which signal a statement and others which signal a query. There are also tunes which allow us to signal which parts of an utterance carry new information in contrast to those which carry only old information. Each intonation pattern has a contour of sounds made at different pitches. It is this contour, rather than any absolute pitch, that is highly significant to the listener. In other words, a tune can be uttered higher or lower and this will not necessarily affect its significance.

More than pitch is involved, for intonation patterns are

systematic and have several components which, as it were, act collectively. As well as pitch they include stress — ways of 'leaning' upon a word to give it prominence for some reason — and pause. Together, pitch, pause and stress constitute an element that is totally lacking from written language. The use of this element is often accompanied by other means of communicating, both vocal and non-vocal, which work only in the face-to-face situations that are typical of the use of spoken language. These include loudness and softness of volume, warm, tender, and soothing qualities of voice and their opposites, and speed of utterance. Among the non-vocal accompaniments are gesture, which may be used to point or to emphasise or to shape, and gaze and expression. When one speaks one tends to use all these systems as well as intonation. They, too, are used in face-to-face situations where verbal and non-verbal feedback is easily taken and where meanings are often about the nearby and the understood rather than about the remote and the strange. It is little wonder, then, that because the transition from being able to speak and listen to being able to read and write involves the child in leaving behind him many familiar ways of getting and giving meanings, it can be a time of confusion and difficulty unless it is handled well by the child's helpers.

Grammar and words

Both modes of language employ grammar and words. In spoken language they are used systematically along with intonation patterns to signal meanings. In written language they take a more prominent part because the systems of intonation disappear and are replaced by other systems such as the orthographic systems of spelling and punctuation which seem to be altogether less salient.

Grammar is probably the most important component of language. The word 'grammar' itself may leave an unpleasant taste in some mouths, particularly if one was in a school which 'did' grammar as part of its language teaching, and more especially if one could not 'do' it very well. 'Doing' grammar was in fact a very odd business. It involved taking language and splitting it up. The language was almost always in the written mode, and always consisted of well-formed sentences. Very often, though, they were not real sentences at all, having been made up especially to be dismembered.

The usual procedure was to divide the sentence into two parts, subject and predicate, and then further to divide each into its constituent parts. The resulting 'analysis' was set out either in little boxes or in a branching diagram.

The hopes of the teacher who 'taught' grammar were three-fold. First it was 'well-known' that doing grammatical analysis of this kind made one better able to read and, more particularly, to write. Secondly, doing grammar was like being put into a sort of mental gymnasium. Grappling with finite verbs and clauses, extensions and enlargements, subjects and objects, complements and adjuncts toned up the mental muscles; the work-out made one brighter. Finally, the work prepared one for learning French or Latin or other languages, for the teacher of these languages would use the concepts gained in the analysis of English as she taught her own language. She, too, felt that it was not just a matter of having a convenient technical vocabulary to talk about language; the understanding gained would be incorporated, indispensably, into the child's new learning.

For the first of these hopes there is no known justification, no evidence that is both supportive and convincing. There is more to be said for the third, but only if the foreign language is taught in a certain way, through grammatical analysis and synthesis, rather on the model of the teaching of a dead language. Many teachers of foreign languages have indeed tried to teach in this way. It is one of the main reasons why this country has an abominable record in getting its young to speak a foreign language after years of being 'taught'.

It is nevertheless likely that there is a truth underlying this mistaken belief in the effectiveness of grammatical analysis. It is this: there can be great advantage in having language to talk about language and this is a theme to which we shall return later. For the moment, it is sufficient to say that the acquisition of language does not require expertise in grammatical analysis of the old sort. Time spent on analysing 'artificial' language or even real language would be better spent in practising to speak or write one's own.

Making play in this fashion with outmoded ideas of the value of grammatical analysis in no way detracts from the supreme importance of grammar as a component of language. There is, indeed, a basic ambiguity in the potential meanings of that term and this needs to be examined. There is 'grammar' which purports to describe a language, or aims at prescribing sets of rules which should govern language use. It is worth noting that both descriptive and prescriptive 'grammars' are themselves articulated in language. But neither of them is the notion with which we are

20

operating. We see 'grammar' as a necessary component of language, one made up of certain systems and categories. They are there whether or not we are articulate about them. Indeed, we may not even be conscious of their presence. Nevertheless, when we use language, we use them. Every competent or partly competent user of a language possesses them in whole or in part.

The *structures* rise in a hierarchy. There are morphemes, words that are made up out of morphemes, groups and clauses that are made out of words, and sentences that are made out of clauses. Above the sentence, there is another level of structure, perhaps more than one level, to which the names 'paragraph' and 'chapter' (in the written mode), 'passage', 'text', and 'discourse' have all been given. *Systems* are located within structures — that is, within words, between words that make up groups and clauses, between clauses that make up sentences and between sentences that make up larger units. There are many systems and they perform many functions. For example, at the word level there are systems that indicate number — singularity and plurality, one and more than one. Take nouns as an example. They have several systems of their own for showing plurality that are different from those of verbs or pronouns. Taking the singular form of the written mode, we can add 's'. Thus 'cat' becomes 'cats'. Another way is to alter the ultimate 'y' to 'i' and then to add 'es'. Several words use 'foreign' systems: 'radius' becomes 'radii', 'phenomenon' becomes 'phenomena', 'tableau' becomes 'tableaux'. Other nouns take a vowel change in the middle. 'Foot' becomes 'feet', 'mouse' becomes 'mice' and so on.* Some words stay the same, as does 'sheep'. Others have two plural forms — 'fish' and 'fishes'. The point is that these ways of indicating the plural are systematic, not haphazard. There are — and this complicates matters — several ways of showing plurality, and the learner has to learn which one is appropriate in any particular case.

There are many such systems in grammar. We shall pick out only a few more examples. One, of great importance, is that of tense. There are three divisions of tenses, past, present and future. Among other things, they allow us to put actions into sequence and to deal with states of affairs. If we were to state the rules for the use and sequencing of tenses we should find them quite complex and this brings us to a very important matter. Children do learn the rules for managing this important part of the grammatical component of language. They do so in the same way as they master most grammatical rules. They learn them in use and not from the precepts of grammar books or teachers.

Aspect is another grammatical system that is closely linked to that of tense. It tells us whether an action is perfective or progressive — the difference exemplified in 'he walked', which is finished, and 'he was walking' which might still be going on.

Mood is another important system in the use of verbs. One can make statements such as 'you are singing', or commands like 'Sing!'. Then there is the conditional, usually introduced by 'if . . .' — which gets us away from facts into another domain of thinking. The same is true of 'might' and 'may' which allow the formulation and expression of speculative thought. Thus verbal systems allow us to deal with what was, what is, what will be, what might be, what could be and much else as well.

What is perhaps the most remarkable grammatical system of all is one that few people seem to be conscious of. It is for putting words into order. The rules for this differ from language to language. In English there is a small number of options, each to be used in appropriate circumstances. One pattern, the most common, is 'subject . . . verb . . . object': 'The man hit the boy.' If we were to take the words uttered by a commentator at a fashion show which were, in random order, 'very', 'this', 'lovely', 'gown' and 'chic', most of us, if asked, could put them into the order in which they were originally spoken. To do so we would have to use our knowledge of word order rules, rules which we know, but could not for the most part put into words. Writers of books on learning English as a second language sometimes take immense trouble to state these rules which are extraordinarily involved and require us to operate a system of categorisation of which most of us are unaware. There are, for example, different categories of adjective, and each has its own privileges of occurrence which determine where it shall stand in relation to other adjectives in the same group of words. When one considers the matter, it is amazing how much grammar we actually know without our necessarily being aware that we do actually know it. We know the 'rules' for using these and many other systems. But we know and have learned them operationally and, most emphatically, not as statements. The thoroughness of the learning can be seen when we consider how rare are the mistakes with word-ordering made even by very young preschool children.

At this stage we can reiterate three important points about grammar. The first is that it is an essential component of language. The second is that it is possible to learn the 'rules' for its use without being articulate about them, without even being aware that the rules

22

exist, for such 'rules' are 'regularities', rather than statements. The third point is that it is necessary to understand that as far as learners are concerned, grammar is an enabling device. It allows them to signal and construe meanings that would be impossible without it.

Finally, we come to words. There is no really clear distinction between words and grammar. Indeed, as we have pointed out, words are a category of grammar. All words have grammatical significance, but some have special importance. The word 'might', for instance, does not label objects in the same way as the word 'table' is said to do, nor does it 'stand for' events in the same way as '(the) shouting' is said to do. Nevertheless it is a very powerful word indeed. The same is true of the word 'if' and the word 'not'. Think of statements such as 'If you turn the tap, water will flow', and 'I shall not accept.' 'If' and 'not' are each strong enough to alter the whole potential meaning of their sentence. They are in no sense words slipped in for a bit of extra colour — as perhaps an adjective might have been.

The point about words is that they are always used in some structure and as part of some system. That structure and that system — what they are part of and what comes before and after — affect their meaning potential. From this point of view, dictionaries are the most misleading books ever written. They purport to indicate what a word means, begging the question of whether any word means anything (something we shall discuss later) and assuming that all words have, at least, an obligatory core of meaning. But what matters is a word's grammatical context and the overall situation in which it is used. It is these that determine what is really 'going on' in a sentence. It is because dictionaries ignore this that so many children find the definitions they give to be so unsatisfactory and bewildering.

It is not only lexicographers who get it wrong, though. It is a common fault to think of language as made up of words — which is very misleading indeed. Words are indeed indispensable, but compared with grammar they are the junior partners. As far as teachers are concerned, it is important that what they try to teach should not be limited, therefore, to matters of vocabulary.

Note

* Of course, this applies only in the written mode. The spoken mode has no spellings at all and any differences are made in sounds.

3

The Development of Speaking
and Listening

The previous chapter analysed the nature of language. This chapter tries to account for the ways in which it is acquired. It is concerned exclusively with the spoken mode and aims at explaining how the various components that constitute language are actually learned and how selections might be made from them and combined to make utterances. It deals at some length with how the speaker, in making his selection, takes into account his audience and the context and situation within which the utterance is to be delivered.

If we had only to deal with the acquisition of sound patterns, words, and grammar, that would be task enough. Learning the sounds is itself very extensive compared with what other species have to learn. Learning the lexicon is also a major business. Already, by the time he reaches school, the child will have learned thousands of words; while he is in the primary school he will learn many thousands more. In learning grammar, he has to take in sets of conventional systems, some of them of considerable complexity and subtlety. But there is more to it than this — more, even than learning to combine these three systems into utterances. For the utterance must signal meanings, and once we take the implications of this into account the complexity of what we have to account for increases immensely.

We can think of language, whether it has been uttered or written, as forming a text. That text can always by analysed in terms of its constituent components. In the case of spoken language, we have already suggested what these should be, though other sorts of analysis are possible. But, however we choose to handle it, text is never the whole of the business. There is always something which stands apart from the text and which acts as a sort of guiding, or defining, principle. 'Discourse' might be a term for this — though most writers use the term to mean something rather different. 'Vein', in the sense of the 'vein' in which something is said, might also be used. Perhaps a better term would be 'key', borrowed from music — a principle and a relationship around which the components of the language are arranged and by means of which appropriate selections from them have been made. Whatever we call it, it is itself the result of certain factors which the speaker needs ideally to take into account as he produces language which will become a text. They include: the sort of meaning he wishes to convey; its purpose; his audience, particularly its size, social status and supposed knowledge; and any other language that is being used by others in a complementary or reciprocal way.

Competence in language is not, therefore, merely a matter of possessing a lexicon, the sound systems and the grammar, together with the ability to put all these together. It is the ability to select elements from these and to combine them into a text which meets other requirements. Putting it another way, making language involves a pragmatic element. If it were not so, speakers would be creating language in a vacuum — which is an impossibility.

It is vital to recognise this pragmatic element because it helps us to define what children must learn. Once its force is admitted, learning language becomes also a matter of learning about the world, including especially the social or interpersonal world, and the constraints that it places on language use. Meaning and communication are both set in this wider context, and it is this wider context that the child must understand for the practical purposes of making language effective. He must allow it to shape both his own language and his understanding of other people's language.

Thus, learning language always involves a breadth of learning that may not have always been readily apparent. What one learns is never really just language items — sounds, words, bits of grammar — so much as the use of systems of which those items are a part. Learning language always extends into learning about the wider world.

The prerequisites of speech

Learning language involves even more than learning about the wider world. It entails learning to do things *in* that world. As we shall see shortly, language comes into the child's productive behaviour much later than do other sorts of communication.

Indeed, one could say that language is a continuation of earlier communication by other means. These other means — language — allow an extension and an amplification of what it is possible to communicate. But language does not appear on the scene fully formed. It has its own antecedents and prerequisites.

For some years some psychologists have been discerning many remarkable abilities in very young children — abilities that seem previously to have been apparent only to adoring mothers and fathers and to doting grandparents. It is now very clear that babies are much more competent than was once generally thought by professional child specialists. They are, for example, much more in touch with their environment than was held to be possible. Indeed, they are not merely in touch with it but actively strive to understand and control it. This seems to be especially true of those parts of their environment which exhibit movement or change. In particular, they seem to be surpassingly interested in those elements in their surroundings that are animate and human. In the longer run, two conditions seem to need to be fulfilled if other humans are to help the process to develop. The first is that they should pay attention to the child. Adult attention is highly motivating, for it gives the child the opportunity to do certain things, and it lends point to doing them. The second is perhaps less predictable: it is that they should lend themselves to the business of being controlled by the child. To an adult, the idea of being controlled by a small baby who is only a few months, or a few days, or a few hours old, may seem to be ridiculous, if only because power seems to be distributed so unequally between the baby and his adult attendant. It is quite certain, though, that bringing out the best in young children, giving them opportunities and allowing them to make the most of them, calls for both understanding and generosity on the part of the adult. The most basic understanding is of what the child needs if he is to develop fully, and the generosity takes the form of a willingness to give him time. In order to help the child to develop, the adult must, then, do some remarkable things. But they are really only remarkable when seen from a certain viewpoint, say that of the uncomprehending alien. From other points of view, that of many parents and, still more perhaps of many grandparents — they seem both natural and obvious. The point for us is that it is in the interactions that are set up very early in life between child and adult that the foundations of future language are to be found.

H.R. Schaffer is among those psychologists who have refused to be blinded by earlier received wisdom, and he has looked afresh at this interaction. Others, such as Jerome Bruner, have gone on to tease out its significance for future language development. Initially, it is worth asserting that these early interactions are not remarkable merely in their own right. Nor is it their sole importance that they are crucial for future language development. They are important also for the development of other aspects of the child's behaviour and competencies. The significance of these newer discoveries for child specialists, for health visitors and for workers in postnatal and antenatal clinics is very great, so great, indeed, that it may eventually call for changes in their training.

It is impossible to consider any child as too young to interact with his environment. The youngest does more than live in it or merely react to it. Even the newborn child demonstrates attributes that should cause any educator to rejoice in anticipation. More than that, even before birth the child is excited by the human voice. Physiological measurements *in utero* seem to show this conclusively. Other physiological measurements, taken soon after birth and under conditions in which he could not possibly have heard it since birth, show that the neonate responds to and recognises his mother's voice. This early interest is maintained and extended. It is followed by a further interest in the human face. Neonates recognise a face as a face from seemingly inadequate data such as when they can only see part of it, or when they are presented with a representation of it that is only partly complete. There is now evidence that by about 8 or 9 months they can even forecast mood from facial expression.

Each year brings further discoveries which extend the range of abilities that we can safely attribute to the very young child. Over the past decade or so, much attention has been paid to the sort of relationship that he builds with his mother (or with another principal caregiver who need not be his biological mother). This is a dyadic relationship which, in its most developed stage, is a twosome of remarkable power, marked by reciprocity and complementarity.

Given the difference in size between them, it is easy to think of the adult as controlling the child. Comforting, attracting attention, changing the mood, lulling the child into somnolence and stimulating him into activity — all are on the list of what we think of as the parent doing to the child. But when the relationship is at its most productive the list of what the child does to the parent is just as extensive. He attracts attention, rewards the parent in various ways; for example, by smiling, he responds, he directs attention to a shared field and so on. Many of these behaviours are deeply rewarding to adults while others, such as crying, though not rewarding, are at least as powerful in their effects.

The essence of the relationship is that it is mutual. The conditions of its success are that the adult should pay frequent attention, should give up her time, and should behave with sensitivity to the moods and the state of wakefulness of the infant. She must be prepared to be influenced and controlled — which simply means that she must let the child play its part as an initiator of joint behaviours. When the relationship is successful, there is no doubt that both partners find it deeply satisfying. It is marked by turn-taking; gaze, posture, touch, vocalisings, all become significant. On the parent's side part of the vocalising takes the form of language. At this stage, the child cannot understand this language in anything like a literal sense. But what he learns from it is deep — that adults use these patterns of sounds (in which, of course, lexis and grammar are clothed or embedded), that they do so using voice colour and intonations that affect him. His own vocalisings increase in response. If he thinks that he is then doing what the adult has done, he is right, though there is more to adult vocalisings than he yet knows.

Given the child's great potential, his consuming interest in voice and face, his willingness to explore, his concern with controlling, we can see that the foundations of linguistic interaction are being laid. The dyadic relationship allows the child to match his behaviour with that of his mother, who makes the whole business easier by, in her turn, matching her behaviour to his. He responds and he initiates. He takes turns. He exchanges vocalisations. And, as we said, the essential condition for this is that he should have found a willing and responsive partner.

Babies coo and cry spontaneously in expressing their feelings. From the developmental point of view, it is vital that sometimes these vocalisings should be responded to. When this happens, their character is transformed. As well as being indicators of the child's emotional state, they begin to mark a rudimentary communicative intent. From this point of view, the stern school of upbringing which advocated the routinising of the child, with regular times for food, sleep, solitariness and so on, did the child a disservice. What was behind it may have been a fear of 'spoiling' the child. But over-rigidity in this way loaded the dice against him by reducing the opportunities for the exercise of the vital mutual relationship. Also, when his crying was persistently ignored, it denied him the occasions, day in and day out, to learn the deep lesson that he could both intend to communicate by his vocalising and also succeed in his intention — as would be evidenced by someone responding to his crying. The moral for parents and for those who advise them is that they should seek all reasonable opportunities from the first moments of the baby's life to make a steady communicating relationship with him. This, above all else, is what sets him on the road to become a successful user of the language.

Teachers will note that these early stages are interpersonal in their nature. From the earliest stages this interpersonal, or social, factor seems to be clearly present. It is so important that it cannot be left to chance. It is the basic, though not the only reason why primary schools need to have a family orientation. The senior partners in the business of language learning are the parents, not the school. Very often they need support and one purpose of the school, in my view, ought to be to give that support.

The roles of parents and the support that the school can give to them, and they to the school, will be another of our recurrent themes. For the moment, however, we return to the business of early language learning.

Babbling

All babies babble. Babbling is the making of sounds repetitively by the young child which starts when the child is a few months old. Its origins are sometimes said to be in pleasurable murmurings — expressions of contentment. From the point of view of learning to speak, it is of the greatest importance.

We adults, being expert, are always likely to underestimate the sheer difficulty of using the body to make the sounds of language. Children, for the most part, show early signs of mastery and this, too, may make us overlook what they actually achieve. It is often a puzzling jolt to adults when 'normal' development does not seem to occur.

Producing language is not merely a matter of using the vocal cords, setting them vibrating, as it were, at will. Even to do this needs control of the breath for it is directing the breath to them that causes them to vibrate. Controlling the breath in turn means controlling the diaphragm. In both cases we are not referring to gross control but to operations that are really quite delicate, at least in the accomplished speaker. The production of sounds that are akin to speech sounds requires, then, a considerable degree of control over the larynx and the breath. It also calls into use the soft palate, the nasal cavity, the dental ridge, the tongue and the lips. All these have to be utilised very delicately not merely in sequence but also in combination. Actually to write down the specifications for the physiological production of various sounds would be a complex operation. What children have to do is to learn to produce such sounds at will, automatically or without seeming to think about them. What we witness when we listen to a baby's babbling is the practice of most complicated physical actions. The degree of accuracy and coordination is of the order that Olympic athletes strive to achieve in their gymnastic competition. If children never accomplished anything else, we should be entitled to wonder at their success in this. Babbling is their spontaneous attempts to gain control over their own vocal and other speech apparatus and to use it to produce at will delicately differentiated sounds. Anyone who still doubts the magnitude of this should suspend for a moment his own automaticity and bring back his production of sounds into conscious consideration. Let him try to make a 'p' sound like that in 'pen'. What happens to the breath? A little puff or explosion? How is this different from when he makes the sound of 'b' as in boat? It is mainly in the use of the larynx, the 'b' sound being what is called 'voiced' in contrast to the 'p' sound which is 'unvoiced'. Let him then try to make the 'm' sound as in 'mat'. Here the nasal cavity comes into use. Then let him try the 'c' as in 'cat'. By now he will realise that none of these simple sounds is really that simple. Finally, let our experimenter bear in mind that the child has to learn to make such sounds using parts of the anatomy that nature really intended for breathing and eating, and not for making sounds at all, or at least so one presumes.

We have said enough to indicate how important babbling is. It is a sort of gymnastic exercise, perhaps best understood as an early example of developmentally important play. But to say that it is important is not to exhaust the topic. For, while babbling seems to begin spontaneously and is apparently the same the world over, it soon loses this spontaneity and becomes different in different parts of the world. The fact is that there are two phases of babbling. The first, we have indicated, seems to be universal. It is universal in two senses. The first is its worldwide identity. The second is that it is characteristic of the development of all normal children. 'Normal' is a difficult word to us. In reality this first phase of babbling is experienced even by many children whom we might not call normal, such as the profoundly deaf and those who are considerably impaired mentally. Handicaps, in short, have to be extremely severe to prevent a child from babbling.

However, the second stage is far from being universal. In it, babbling in England begins to differ from babbling in France or in any other linguistic community. The sounds that are now being practised are those of the mother tongue. It is not the case that one stage stops abruptly and is then replaced by the other; the two merge and sounds that are constituents of the mother tongue gradually come into prominence. At this point babbling ceases to be universal. Whether a child enters this stage at all depends on whether he can *hear* the sounds around him. By 'hear' we do not mean simply 'overhear', for success depends on language being directed to him. Deaf children who cannot hear them at all do not enter this phase, nor do children who are totally isolated and neglected.

'Babbling one', then, as we might call the first phase, is spontaneous and universal; 'Babbling two' is language-specific and entry to it depends on being a hearing member of a particular language community. In other words, even such an apparently solitary activity is now socially determined. Moreover, the amount of babbling at this stage seems to depend on how much language the child hears and particularly on how often he is engaged in being spoken to. Again, the immense importance of prelinguistic interpersonal interactions becomes obvious.

The stages of babbling coincide with the development of two other capabilities both of which are specifically and directly important for language learning. The first of these is the growth of the child's ability to use intonation patterns. Such patterns, it is likely, are invented by the child himself in the first place. At least, the actual tunes are invented but not, perhaps, the idea of using them for this may or may not be spontaneous. It could be that it begins spontaneously and then is reinforced and altered as the child hears and notices that other people use them. What now happens in the educating family is really very remarkable, for these tunes are invested with meaning, not so much by the utterer as by the listener. Fond mums and dads either find or pretend to find meaning in them. This attribution of meaning is probably the occasion of some very significant deep learning in the child. If the penny has not yet dropped that his vocalisings can be meaningful to others, it will do so now. Furthermore, this will nurture that idea which, hopefully, is growing from other activities as well — that it is possible to *intend* to make meanings. In this way it is likely that intention, too, is as much social, or interpersonal, in origin as is speech itself.

Be that as it may, the growth of intentionality in the child is one of the great underlying conditions which must be fulfilled if he is to become a successful learner and user of language.

The stages of babbling coincide, indeed they merge, with a second development, also of great significance. This is the growth of protoconversations. These occur when there is an interchange which resembles that of a true conversation, characterised by turn-taking. Protoconversations are relatively protracted, involving several continuing exchanges. They take place with an adult, as a rule, largely because only when one partner is adult is there likely to be enough skill to maintain the exchanges. Needless to say, the most likely partner will be the mother. What usually happens is that the mother either initiates or responds to contributions from the infant. She will herself use language, usually one of a series of variants at her command which we call 'motherese'. The child responds using intonation patterns and elements from his own babblings. The exchanges are generally accompanied by eye contact and, often, by smiling.

Thus we can say that when things have gone well, and particularly when there has been frequent and ample interaction with adults, some essential learning of quite remarkable kinds will have been completed by the end of the babbling stage. First, there will have been a protracted period in which mother and child each tries to key in their behaviours to the other. This is the time when the mother must be a willing partner, lending herself to purposes which the child desires and anticipating the ways in which his behaviour and his wishes are moving. Then in several ways the child's utterances become invested with some sort of meaning. Crying and cooing are both responded to, opening the way to their use as communication and not merely as expressive devices. Babbling, that amusing and extraordinary phenomenon, then begins. When all is conducive, this then extends into a second phase in which the basic sounds, some of the phonemes of the language, are practised with great frequency and regularity. At the same time, the child begins to use intonation patterns and to employ them in conversation-like encounters with others.

This is still the prelinguistic stage of development. The child cannot speak a word of his mother tongue. What he can do is to listen to it. How much, and what sorts of, meaning he derives from it is not sure. Probably he receives affective messages — those which signal a stage of mind and reassurance and comfort. But he has already learned a great deal about what language is and something about how it works. He knows, too, about communication and the basis of intentionality, on which depends so much of his future development — cognitive, social and emotional, as well as linguistic — is already laid. What is missing is his own production of language, but when things have gone well he is now superbly placed to tackle that.

Learning the mother tongue

The first words that children use are usually naming words, but they are not used merely for naming, or at least not for long. They are soon employed in the service of the old, prelinguistic communicative functions of protesting, requesting, directing attention and so on. Words, that is, are soon put to communicative purpose. This is the real root of grammatical structures that are longer than the word. At first the word may have to carry an enormous burden. 'Dolly', for example, may mean 'There is a dolly,' 'There is my dolly,' 'Look at the dolly,' or 'Give me that dolly.' Structures expand into two-word utterances and as they do the use of this new grammatical structure allows the child to become a little more explicit. At the same time, the child is learning how to use his limited resources in a social world, for social reasons.

Some investigators consider that some children are primarily referrers, particularly taken up with the business of naming, and that other children are from the start more expressive, by which they mean that the child is inclined to getting things done in a social context by means which include language. If this is so, it does not take long for the two paths to converge, and development proceeds as both referring and expressing or managing. From the point of view of the parent, the essentials for the healthy development of the child seem to be, first, a willingness to give him time and attention; second, a willingness to communicate and be communicated with; and third a keenness to put the child into certain circumstances in which the use of language is both favoured and is likely to be of significance to him. These circumstances might include ritualistic games like handing objects back and forth, going into new environments, dealing with new objects and toys (when the names for the objects and processes involved are introduced), and sessions looking at and talking about books and pictures. But in all these situations the key factor is the willing adult. There is good reason to believe that it is the presence of this willing adult that determines or strongly influences the success of the child in the whole business of learning language. It seems very likely that those children who are often thought of as being linguistically 'deprived' may have missed this vital agency in their upbringing.

When development is satisfactory the child develops a great appetite for names, even to the point of being tiresome to adults. From the child's point of view, the possession of the name for a person, animal, object or action is the first step in controlling it. Once he knows the name, he can use his very limited powers over grammar and, later, his more fully developed grammatical knowhow to get things done over a wider range than had ever been possible by merely pointing or gazing.

The learning of grammar goes on very rapidly. Systems such as negation he soon acquires and, with negation, the multi-purpose 'No' which is so powerful even without any naming words to go with it. He also acquires other systems such as questioning, often beginning by using an intonation device with the words still in a 'normal' order.

I have some?

and

You like this?

said with a rising pitch.

Then an appropriate auxiliary is used, but still with the question being signalled by rising intonation rather than by a change in word order:

We can go out?

In the child's third year he will be tackling what are known as 'wh' questions. These are questions which cannot usually be answered with a 'yes' or 'no'. They begin with 'wh' words such as 'where', 'when', 'what', 'why', and their close cousin, 'how'. Such questions also use an auxiliary. Some children put it after the subject before trying the adult's positioning, which is before the subject. Thus they might say:

Where you are going?

and move on later to

Where are you going?

And so the story continues. By the time he is 5, the child has possession of most of the grammatical systems of the language, though he is not equally secure in the use of them all and some, like the passive voice, will probably take several years more before they, too, are safely included in his repertoire.

In all this learning there is one feature that the teacher should be conscious of. It is one that grammarians have tended to ignore, leaving the implication that children, having learned the grammar by the age of 6 or 7 (with some exceptions) have really little else to learn. Possession of a grammatical system, however, is not the end of the story, either in the task of comprehending someone else's language or in producing one's own. The child needs to know the purposes for which a word in a grammatical system can be used and the circumstances in which it is appropriate to use it — what we have called the pragmatics. Finally, he needs also to acquire ease and fluency in using it. Thus the old habit of investigators, who were often satisfied when a child gave some evidence of possessing an item or a system really will not do for teachers. What they and the school have to do is to bring ease and fluency into the child's use of his expanding grammatical and lexical systems.

In what we have said up to now we have presumed cognitive growth, taking the position that, on the whole, cognitive growth (which itself may be partly social or interpersonal) precedes the use of particular language. This, however, needs to be qualified. It will be referred to again in Chapter 7 which deals with the place of language in learning. Here, it is necessary to insist that the employment of grammar or of lexical items does not necessarily denote possession of the fuller understanding of them which we might expect in adults.

The use of 'because' as a conjunction which also signals a cause-and-effect relationship is an illustration of this. What children grasp is one part of its use before they understand the other. Thus they may use 'because' in a well-wrought and meaningful sentence without intending to indicate this cause-and-effect relationship, having stopped short at the point where they understood properly only its use as a conjunction. In time, their understanding will 'fill out' and their initial, limited, use of 'because' needs to be seen in its proper light as a step in the right direction.

Many words are used with only partial understanding. For example, one does not need to have a fully developed concept before one begins to use the class name for the concept. In other words, a noun may be used when there is incomplete understanding of its meaning potential. The same is true for other parts of speech. It is not surprising that this should be characteristic of children's language, for it also applies frequently in adult language. An instance of this might be the use of the word 'vehicle' by an adult. Most adults would understand that 'vehicle' is a name given to a superordinate category which, by definition, embraces several subordinate categories. Most of them could easily give examples of these subordinate categories. 'Cars' and 'bicycles' would spring to mind. Now, the characteristic of a class is that all members share one or more criterial attributes. They all have something in common and it is that which makes them a class. The same applies to a superordinate category: all the members are classes, each with its own defining characteristic. This is another way of saying that all cars have something in common, as do all bicycles and that in their capacity as vehicles cars have something in common with bicycles. So far so good. Most adults feel that they 'just know' what vehicles are without being able necessarily to define the term. However, a problem arises when new candidates are proposed for inclusion. Does a 'bus' have the defining attribute that would allow us to count it as a 'vehicle'? Most would answer that it does. The same applies to 'motor scooter'. But does it apply to 'tractor', to 'tank', to 'boat', to 'aeroplane'? Many of us might find some difficulty with the last three items. The characteristics which we suppose to define a class and therefore to define the word for that class are often uncertain round the edges. Vehicle is not an isolated example. Take three words that are close to each other in what they are held to signify: 'palace', 'castle', and 'fort'. Try to explain the differences between them. We could go some way to doing so, but there will always be some examples that do not fit our classes at all definitely. Of course, for most everyday purposes, adults can handle the differences quite comfortably without even being aware that there are problems. The child's plight is essentially different. Language must seem to him to be much more plastic: re-establishing boundaries and finding out in what circumstances and for what purposes words and expressions may be used is the heart of the language game. As long as he is not put off the game either by constant defeat or through chronic neglect, the child will succeed, always provided he is working on solid foundations.

The crucial role of the situation in which language is used and of the principle that language needs to be learned in use in situations can be illustrated in many ways. The learning of relational terms is a case in point. Such words as 'big' and 'little', 'tall' and

'short', 'thick' and 'thin', 'deep' and 'shallow', have potential
meanings that are determined to a quite spectacular extent by the
circumstances in which they are used and particularly by what it
is they qualify. Thus a 'big' ball is a great deal smaller than a 'small'
field; a 'big' bush as a rule is smaller than a 'small' tree; a 'tall'
boy may or may not be taller than a 'short' man; a 'thick' slice
of bread is probably much thinner than a 'thin' man and so on.
Such words as 'here' and 'there', beloved of many writers of early
reading books, may also be relational. What is 'here' to one person
may be 'there' to another. We can imagine a child trying to get
his mind round a situation in which one adult may say to him 'Come
here' and another adult, in a different part of the room may also
say 'Come here'. If the child obeys first the one and then the other
of the identical-sounding instructions, it may involve him in moving
in diametrically opposed directions. The same might not be true
if each adult had said 'Go there', for then they might both have
meant the same place. In print such words may have a further
meaning potential which is in fact to act as a formula with which
to open a certain sort of sentence: 'There was once a beautiful
princess.' The point, of course, is that 'simple' words are not always
really simple. They may often involve the child in doing a great
deal of sorting out over a period of time.

One could go on multiplying examples but enough has been said
to make the point. In the preschool and early school years the child
has to become adept at taking information from the situation as
a whole, from both its physical and social dimensions, from relationships between the speaker and hearer, between one event and
another and between one statement and another. In these senses,
learning language is also learning about the world and about human
relations.

Before we finally isolate some of the main goals for the language
programme we could perhaps distil two principles out of this discussion. The first concerns context. Children always and only learn
language in a context. From their point of view, the very meaning
of the language depends on that context, and as was pointed out
above, early language is only one part of ongoing action. It may,
for instance be a sort of running commentary and not intended for
communicative purposes, or it may be deeply embedded in a totality
along with other communicative actions such as gaze, gesture,
pointing, reaching and so on. In a sense the child has to learn
to decontextualise it. This process involves segmenting it or, in
other words, being able to distinguish separate words inside whole

expressions. Once they have been distinguished they can be detached and taken and used in other appropriate situations. Just as language needs to be distinguishable from other sorts of behaviour, so within language, grammar needs to be recognised so that it too may be reapplied. The principle that we are after is something like this: although language is learned from situations and is always met in contexts to which it gives and from which it takes, meaning, it is necessary for the child to learn that the connection between language and situation is of a particular sort, so that language can be detached from the situation in which it is found and then, as it were, re-used in different situations. The hard part is not merely learning the words and grammar but understanding the conventions which govern this re-use and which stretch deep into the world of objects, events and human relationships.

To this is linked a second principle and it concerns the combining of strings of language to make structures. In both conversation and extended monologue the child, if he is to be successful, needs to be able to perceive what sort of use he is engaged upon and to act accordingly. For example, is it playful or an invitation to play? Is it serious, perhaps calling for close attention? Is it managerial? Or teasing? Or ironical?

As I pointed out earlier, there is an analogy between language and music, bringing the notion of 'key' into prominence. Understanding what 'key' language should be in determines the choice of language. What the child is doing is learning what the American, James Moffett, called 'the world of discourse'. Learning this world involves subtle understandings of what I call 'key', the ability to understand language and to produce language for some purpose that might be either obvious or ulterior.

There is another feature of discourse that we should stress. It is that it usually involves the making of stretches of language and not just single utterances. These stretches take two basic forms, monologue and dialogue, in which case the classical form is of initiation and response. In monologue, a single person has responsibility for making a text. In dialogue, in contrast, two participants act together to construct a text that both will regard as meaningful. What one person says depends in several ways on what has been said before.

In the following extract from a transcript a teacher is talking to a young infant, Mark, who is in his first few months in school. They are talking about a book, in which the main character is Donk.

1. *Teacher* Find Donk. You start off by telling me the story of Donk.
2. *Mark* Once . . .
3. *Teacher* That's it. Ready?
4. *Mark* Why, does it say Donk on it?
5. *Teacher* Yes, there. That says Donk. You see if you can tell me that story.
6. *Mark* Here is Donk. Next to . . . . Here is a field. Donk who lives in the field.
    There's a little boy next to the field.
7. *Teacher* Ummm.
8. *Mark* He likes to ride on Donk's back.
9. *Teacher* Ummm.
10. *Mark* A little man walked into the field. And the Little Donk said hee-haw, hee-haw.

There are several features in this exchange that are worthy of notice. Accompanying notes, supplied by the teacher, reveal that there were several interesting voice changes in Mark's language. The circumstances were that the teacher had read the story to the class, that Mark himself was unable to read and that he was thus working from memory. The whole dialogue illustrates the opportunities that books provide for extending spoken language. Our present concern, however, is more specifically with key, with the way (to put it rather differently) that Mark tunes in and quickly comes to understand what is wanted of him. He finds this out not just from the language that the teacher uses but also from the surrounding context: the two were alone, the book from which he had seen the teacher read, was open. He was used to sessions in which the two of them conversed. Thus he drew on his personal knowledge of situation in order to understand. He comes to understand that he should read the story, though he may have wondered why, since the teacher was clearly familiar with it. In line 1 the teacher initiates. In line 2 Mark responds quite appropriately in the sense that he is following her instructions and that he has used a standard formula opening very suitable for the telling and retelling of stories. In line 3 the teacher interrupts him, at the same time confirming his choice of 'wavelength' or 'key'. Mark is then willing to play the interruption game and changes role somewhat by seizing the initiative. Instead of merely responding, he now seeks to make the teacher respond — the essence of what we shall refer to later as 'mutualised conversation'. On this occasion, the teacher was not willing to play this particular game and so in line 5 she answers him but takes back the initiative by again asking him to tell the story. Again, Mark responds. Again, he uses language that he thinks is appropriate and which is often found in early reading books: 'Here is Donk. . . . Here is a field.' Then he loses his hold on such 'literary' language as he tackles the job of conveying meaning. 'Donk who lives in the field' is an utterance that could only live in this sort of context. It is not a well-wrought sentence, being more of a labelling device to introduce a character whom both can see before them on the page. And so Mark goes on, listening for other information. The whole gets its unity mainly from its thematic concerns. In other words, the language makes very good sense in the circumstances. And the principal features of the circumstances are that Mark has been asked to retell a story and that he is doing so with the book open. On the whole, one could say that Mark is communicating very successfully indeed. The encounter goes on:

10. *Mark* A little man walked into the field. And the Little Donk said hee-haw, hee-haw.

At this point there was an interruption as a child came into the room.

11. *Teacher* Come and listen to the story. Start again, Mark. Come and listen very quietly. Mark's telling us a story.
12. *Mark* Here is Donk. Donk lives in a field. A little boy lived in this field. He liked to ride on Donk's back. One day a little man came into the field. He walks into this field. Little Donk. . . . Little Donkey laughs. The man walks and the grass goes red. The little man runs and the grass goes blue. The little man jumps over the fence and the little man goes yellow. Donk eat some . . . mm. . . red grass . . . and . . . now umm when the little boy . . . now you're too fat for me to ride on.
13. *Teacher* (Laughs)
14. *Mark* And so he ate some blue grass . . . . He got thinner.
15. *Teacher* (Laughs)
16. *Mark* And the little boy said — You too thin for me to ride on you . . . then he took some yellow grass.

It is worth noticing how quickly Mark picks up his new instructions. He does not merely repeat what he has said before. He gets the salient meanings into his language as he did before, but now the language is changed. He also becomes more fluent. There are two probable reasons for this. The first is that he has already had a first shot and this is a second, and if the second is not a repetition of the first, at least he feels that he has solved his communication problems and can now make his points with modified language. The second is that his task is now much more realistic, in the sense that telling a story to someone who has previously read it to you is a slightly odd assignment. The teacher got over it by creating an atmosphere in which she suggested by her involvement and her obvious enjoyment that it was a pleasure for her to be reminded of the story. But there were stronger reasons for telling it the second time. The child who interrupted had not heard the story before. This brought about a more realistic situation in that it now posed one of the problems that is present in all conversations — which is that the speaker must estimate how much knowledge he can assume the listener to have. This is a problem of which children gradually become aware in the process of speaking and listening. Making the right assessment is both risky and skilful. It rests on assumptions, some of which could be wrong. It requires a speaker who is skilful enough to pay attention to any feedback, verbal and non-verbal, and who, having assessed what adjustments need to be made, can then shape his language in order to make them.

What we have in the second phase of this encounter is something that is lacking in the first. It is what we call a 'long utterance'. In the transcript it is uninterrupted for about six lines. This brings us again to a problem that is present in all language but which becomes more urgent in long utterances. It comes down to this: how is the language to hold together? What is to cement it? What is to make it a unity? As we have indicated previously, there are two aspects to this problem — the thematic and the linguistic, matters of coherence and matters of cohesion. The first is solved by ordering the content in the same way as it would have occurred in real time. In other words, on this occasion and very appropriately for telling a story, the child adopts the chronological principle of organisation. Problems of cohesion between utterances but within the long utterance itself are as yet not solved and are probably not even fully recognised by the child. Yet in line 8 we have a pronominal reference back from 'he' to 'the little boy'. Such reference back to something already mentioned overtly is called *anaphoric reference*. It is an important cohesive device, and the child is on his way to mastering it.

It is worth noting that as the long utterance progressed, it became less coherent and less cohesive. Perhaps Mark was getting tired. He was certainly working hard and successfully, dealing with several matters at once. It is almost as though at the end his willingness to develop his tale is overruled by his anxiety to get on to the punch lines and to miss out nothing that was salient. In the event that is exactly what he does. A similar thing is often to be seen when young children retell jokes. They are so anxious to get to the funny bit that it overpowers everything else — a fault, perhaps, but not a grievous one, something which perhaps could be seen not as a fault but as a stage on the way to new levels of communicative competence.

The goals of the spoken language element

The sketch above has taken us from early prelinguistic behaviour through the acquisition of lexis, grammar and intonation patterns to their combination and use in different contexts. Much has been made of the interpersonal nature of language and it has been established as a principle that the learner must take into account many features of the situation as he composes his language. In particular, it has been stressed that it is wrong to take a view of language which deals only with the inner components of language and that any theory of language must take into account its complex relationships with context and situation. It follows that any theory of language learning or language teaching must take the same considerations into account. Learning to speak and listen is, therefore, always a matter of using language as it functions in real situations and with real people; it is not merely a business of learning words and grammar.

There is more to it than that, of course. The production of language involves considerations of coherence and cohesion, in short of unity, and these matter greatly in longer utterances.

With this in mind, we suggest that there are several goals that schools need to adopt to guide their work in spoken language. If, however, 'goals' signal notions of 'destination', we have used the wrong term, for what we wish to indicate is directions in which to go rather than places to reach. These directions are appropriate for all primary children and, indeed, for older children and adults, too, for in principle we each of us could go further in these directions than we have actually gone. None of us is 'learned up' in the business of using language.

Underlying the idea of goals or directions is the notion of communicative competence. This involves being able to put meanings into language, meanings for different purposes, aimed at different sorts of audiences, about different subject matters. It also involves the receptive, but highly active, skills of listening, that is of construing meanings made by different people, in different circumstances, over a wide range of subject matters. This, of course, expresses the level of competence at a high level of generality. Before it can be useful to teachers, it needs to be put into more practicable forms. Accordingly, we shall first of all list the directions in which the child's language should be developed. Then we shall discuss some of the techniques for fostering language and the difficulties that might accompany them in practice. Finally, we shall look ahead to the later years of the primary school to amplify and extend what has been said.

First then to the goals or directions. They aim to get the child

(1) to use language for many purposes and, particularly, with reference 'beyond the here and now';
(2) to use language in mutualised conversations.*
(3) to develop long utterances;
(4) to develop also the listening skills that will enable him to construe meanings when others use language for the above purposes.

These goals are to be taken as furthering the achieving of communicative competence. In other words, they are more specific instances of the ways in which language can be used both to signal and to construe ranges of meaning concerned with different topics in diverse circumstances.

Language for many purposes and 'beyond the here and now'

We stressed above the need to understand that, while language always occurred in a situation of some sort, it was not indissolubly bound to that situation; that, while language is always learned in a situation, it is important for the learner to grasp the twin principles that language should always be appropriate to that situation and that elements of language, once learned, can be used in other situations, provided that the rules of appropriateness are observed.

Such understanding does not come immediately. When language is used at first, both when it is heard and when it is spoken, it is part of the action. In the child's early days, it is not always easy for the listener to tell what is language and what is something else. Gradually, however, language attains a measure of autonomy. Its links with situation change. It can be perceived as something separable from other sorts of behaviour. Those grammatical rules for combining language come to be used as rules for recombining language.

A major part of using language is bound up with the creation of joint fields of reference which the speaker shares with the listener. The establishment of such fields dates from prelinguistic times, when the child becomes quite skilled both at referring to objectives (through gazing, pointing and reaching), getting others to pay attention to them, and, when he wants, getting something done about them — such as having them reached and handed to him by someone else. These skills are continued into the linguistic era. Much early language is in fact an extension of pointing by other (linguistic) means.

Language is at this point very much concerned with the 'here and now', that is, with objects, events and persons in the immediately perceptible environment. It is a major advance when it comes to be used to refer to objects, events and people outside those immediate surroundings. There is no doubt that the child learns to listen to such references before he can begin to use them himself. As people engage him in their talk, such references intrude. The range of attention that he shares with the speaker widens. He begins to understand more about the use of words. Appropriate ways of talking about the imaginary and the remote are introduced to him. He begins to leave far behind his use of language mainly as a means of pointing, for what is now being referred to cannot be pointed at.

Using language to go 'beyond the here and now' also has consequences for mental growth. The world of joint attention is being extended. The child is required to take account in his mental structures not only of things he has actually experienced as real events, but of things and matters quite remote, not present in his memory, being introduced to him for the first time. We shall take this further in Chapter 7 which deals with the place of language in learning. For the present, it is enough to note that extending the range of reference and attention in this way places great burdens on the child both cognitively and linguistically. That is why parents and teachers need to manage the process with care and sympathetic insight.

Going 'beyond the here and now' entails using language for

many purposes. In this regard it is important for teachers to leave
far behind them any notion that that language is monolithic. In
Chapter 2 we pointed out the existence of varieties of language such
as dialects. Here we are concerned with other sorts of variation.
For example, there is register, which I take to be the particular uses
of language as it is concerned with a particular occupation or subject. Car mechanics talk quite differently in their professional
capacity from the ways that brain surgeons talk in theirs. Teachers
use words that are not wholly exclusive to them but which cluster
in their language. Thus we should expect them not to talk, typically,
of 'gaskets' or of 'hemispheric functionings' but of 'attendance',
'attainment', 'intelligence' and so on. We should note, too, that
the manifestations of register go beyond the merely lexical and take
in whole ways of speaking. Thus when a teacher asks, 'Can you
hear a noise?' it means 'Be quiet.' 'Have you finished yet?' may
mean 'Get on with your work,' and 'George, we don't do that sort
of thing, do we?' was Joyce Grenfell's delicious way of poking fun
at our language and the way we use it.

The point to remember is that subjects and occupations attract
their own distinctive ways of speaking. This is one aspect of using
language for different purposes. It may sound as though register
is an adult concept but it concerns children very much. Mothers
use their own register in talking to very young children — they
heighten the pitch, talk more slowly and loudly, and use fairly simple
grammar, making one point at a time, particularly when they want
their child to cotton on. And so, from the cradle and increasingly
through school, the child encounters these specialist uses, all of them
influenced by the contexts in which they appear. By the time he
gets to school, at the very latest, he must begin to operate them.
For example, if he does not use the approved register when he wants
to go to the lavatory, he may create consternation. The same may
apply if he swears. It might be permissible at home, but it will certainly be frowned on by teachers in school.

Using language for different purposes, though, entails more than
just using appropriate registers. It goes much wider. There are uses
of language which reoccur in many contexts. This is the truth that
Joan Tough confronted in her work for the Schools Council which
was intended to help teachers to foster the spoken language skills
of nursery and infant children. She understood, and then did a great
deal to persuade teachers, that language was not monolithic, that
it was used for many purposes, and that it was necessary that
children should have experience in both listening to and speaking

language that was to be used for different purposes.

Accordingly, she suggested a classification that divided such uses into seven classes. The division was to be used both as a basis for describing children's language and for fostering it. Each of the seven uses was accompanied by a list of 'strategies' which did not so much define the use as indicate different ways of expressing meaning that serve particular uses. Broadly, the object was to get the children to use these strategies. In order to assist the teacher to do this, Tough suggested a further class of dialogue strategies which were devices of one sort and another that the teacher could use to foster, in turn, the child's language uses.

Tough's classification of uses, together with some of the attendant strategies for the child to adopt, were:

(1) *self-maintaining*: referring to physical and psychological needs; protecting the self; justifying behaviour and claims;

(2) *directing*: monitoring and directing one's own actions and those of others and collaborating in action with others;

(3) *reporting on past and present experiences*: labelling, referring to detailed incidents, making comparisons, recognising related aspects, making analyses and reflecting on the meanings of experiences, including one's own feelings;

(4) *towards logical thinking*: explaining a process, recognising causal and dependent relationships; recognising problems and their solutions; justifying judgements; recognising principles, etc.;

(5) *predicting*: anticipating and forecasting events, predicting the consequences of actions and events, etc.;

(6) *projecting*: into the feelings, experiences and reactions of others, and into situations never experienced;

(7) *imagining*: developing an ordinary situation based on real life or on fantasy; developing an original story.

There are surely consideration merits in any classification which impresses on teachers that there is a diversity of uses and that children need practice and experience in a wide range of them. It might be possible to criticise Tough's list on several grounds — that it is not comprehensive, that there is no question of grading or progression about it, that many of the categories and their attendant strategies are cognitive (recognising causal and dependent relationships is an example), rather than linguistic. Furthermore, the list, it could be said, pays no attention to the components which make up language — to grammar, for example, or lexis, or intonation or to their selection, combination and use. Neither, it could be added, are the uses presented in ways which are sensitive to situations. They leave discourse and related ideas such as 'keying in' or 'tuning in' quite unconsidered. Nevertheless, these are not equally serious criticisms; none, except the last is really damaging and the value of Tough's list in pointing to the diversity of language use is undiminished.

However, Tough's dialogue strategies, which are to be used by the teacher, are open to more serious objection. The categories are:

(1) *orientating strategies*: utterances, questions and comments that set a child's thinking towards a particular topic and use of language and invite the child to respond;

(2) *enabling strategies*: for following through, focusing and checking;

(3) *informing strategies*: by which the child is given information, explanations and facts as he needs them;

(4) *sustaining strategies*: comments that support the child and ensure him of the listener's attention;

(5) *concluding strategies*: which signal the intention to close either the dialogue or a particular phase of it before opening another topic.

Tough recognises that there may be other strategies but claims that the ones in the list are the important ones, 'since these reflect the part the teacher must play in promoting the child's skills of thinking and using language'. Perhaps the severest criticism of these strategies is to say that they are likely to result in catechetical interviews between the teacher and the child, with the teacher in the role of initiator and the child in that of responder. This brings us close to the heart of the matter, for many of the most rewarding and fruitful exchanges between adult and child are those where the conversation is not dominated by the teacher in this way. This is not to say that the teacher does not exercise ultimate control, for she does — but in a subtle way. Some of the video tapes prepared by Tough show teacher-child interchange at a low level with the teacher trying hard to employ her dialogue strategies and the child utterly dominated by her. The result is a travesty of what fruitful conversation should be.

This is connected with a further criticism. In Tough's scheme the child is given little guidance on how to conduct a conversation, how to start it, how to finish it or how to sustain it. The model that is offered is that of the teacher's own methods and these, we have claimed, are not good — even for the teacher. They would be worse for the child.

The fact is that talk is always dependent upon human relations, while human relationships, in turn, depend on language. Human relationships, that is, affect talk and are affected by it. It follows that any programme which is intended to foster children's talk should first of all pay attention to the prevailing climate in the classroom and particularly to the quality and style of the human relationships that are being built there.

The use of language by the teacher is partly determined by the need to manage her class, to establish order, to initiate and conclude phases of activity, to get children from one place to another, to maintain discipline, and so on. The dilemma she has to face is this: such language is, at one and the same time, both necessary and counterproductive. There must be management and language is indispensable to it. Nevertheless, on the whole it works against the sort of relationship and the sorts of language that are needed to flourish in that relationship. It may also encourage children to switch off their attention. There are partial solutions to the dilemma. The first and most important requirement is to keep management talk to the absolute minimum. Routines help greatly and, as most nursery and infant teachers know, the quiet word to an individual is often more effective than general instructions, admonitions and warnings addressed to the whole class. A further solution rests on the degree of priority given to conversation. Conversation on a mutualised basis is really very important for three main reasons: in the first place it enhances the quality of human relationships. Then it provides a good model of conversation management together with the opportunity to practise it; finally, its particularly intricate dynamics allow a flexibility which is essential if encounters are to be profitable socially, intellectually, and linguistically. It is the interplay of one mind with another, and thus of one string of language with another, that negotiates the meanings and significances conducive to growth.

From this it follows that such conversations should be staple diet, not least in the early years of schooling. It further follows as a negative conclusion that language and relationships which are not helpful should be changed. There are two more implications. The first is that the importance of conversation should be impressed upon parents; the second is that the whole organisation of the school, of the way the teacher actually spends her time, and of the role of parents inside the school may need to be re-examined.

Earlier in this section, the reader was reminded of the two-way relationship between language and human relations. There is another two-way relationship which is also important for our purposes; that between curriculum, taken at its widest, and language. Curriculum provides opportunities for the use of language, and language provides a major means of achieving the ends of the curriculum. From this it might be easy to see that a programme of 'talk', disconnected from the wider purposes and opportunities of the curriculum would lose much of its point and most of its strength. From the point of view of language development, there is an absolute need for a curriculum which engages the full interest of the child. If what is experienced is boring, then it is hardly worth talking about. On the contrary, the child will want to forget it and not to 'go on' about it. In contrast, if there are new experiences, new materials, new places, new people, new principles to explore, the use of language will be properly stimulated. Much of this constitutes a case for our second goal which is the use of language in mutualised conversations. More will be said about it below. Looking ahead, we can say that having categories of language that one wants to pursue, is one thing, but that setting up the right experiences and building the human relations that will nurture language are quite another. There are interconnectons — as we have pointed out language both depends upon and furthers human relationships and curriculum process and in order to achieve viable goals we have, so to speak, to shunt to and fro, first paying attention to one side and strengthening each as we go on.

Children's language grows in successful schools. Successful schools have a feeling of buoyancy about them — a feeling that life is exciting, that new experiences await in abundance, that one is an explorer, that school is an enjoyable place to be. A 'buoyant' school is a place where children become engaged — deeply engrossed — in their pursuits. In such a school, the conditions for learning — cognitive, emotional, social and linguistic — are optimal. A sense of realism demands that we recognise that not all schools can be like this for all of the time. But it is important that they should try to be. When they do, the demands they make on language and the opportunities that they afford for learning language are quite different from those that bore children with seeming irrelevancies.

It is obvious that the richer and more varied the experiences, the more call there will be to learn and use new words. It is perhaps less obvious that there will also be powerful influences on the use of grammar. Let us take interrogation as an example. Earlier, we made the point that most children 'possess' the several ways of asking questions early in their school careers. But 'possession' is not the same as ease and fluency of use. And ease and fluency come about not through any parrot-like repetition of forms but through responding successfully to constraints that are set up in the lifestyle. From the child's point of view, any experiments that he makes in using interrogatives are not principally to further his linguistic prowess. Their purpose is not linguistic at all. It is the need to find out that is the governing factor. When this is present, all he wants is a model — a set of examples met as part of a rich linguistic environment and, later on, feedback to give him an idea of how successful he has been.

And so we could go on. The content of our list of uses is determined by the curriculum. The rich curriculum in the buoyant school will certainly cover all the uses in Joan Tough's list. It will also get the child to use language for such diverse purposes as finding out, persuading, giving instructions, planning, and so on.

Language in mutualised conversations

All conversations are marked by some degree of reciprocity. It takes two to converse and at any one time there must be an initiator and a responder. Their contributions are complementary and are characterised by that turntaking which had its roots in prelinguistic days. A 'mutualised' conversation is one in which there is role change. For part of the time the initiator becomes the responder and the original responder becomes the initiator and takes the main responsibility for the management and the direction of the conversation. When a truly mutualised conversation takes place the benefits which come from the nature of conversation itself tend to be enjoyed by both partners. If we list its attributes we shall be able to see that it does indeed offer a unique set of opportunities:

(1) *attention*: partners in a conversation have to pay attention to each other and to whatever is being talked about;
(2) *understandings*: these are not merely transmitted from one person to another, although that may frequently happen. There is also a possibility that they will be negotiated in the course of give and take. The result of this would be that one partner does not merely 'take over' understandings from the other

50

partner; he finds his way to new understandings which may be different both from those that he started with and from his partner's.

(3) *feedback*: conversation is by its nature an exercise in speaking and listening. Its mechanics allow opportunities that would be rarely found elsewhere to receive feedback pertaining to both skills. Feedback to the teacher is, of course, different from that to the child. Each may learn a great deal about the other;

(4) *model*: successful language use is always a model for the child. In the course of his talk he will gradually learn how others manage the business — how they start and stop, how they link, how they change role from initiator to responder and back again, and so on;

(5) *values*: conversation is a way of demonstrating to the child that he is valued. For the teacher to give him her attention is a practical testimony to that effect. To pay attention to what a child says and to engage in a give-and-take, which is the essence of conversation, is a way of boosting the child's self-esteem.

For these reasons we may look upon conversation as a golden road. Its worth to the child goes far beyond the linguistic. For the teacher, though, it raises problems of time and organisation. If conversation is to be successful, it demands skill and, as the child's skill grows, he will be able to turn increasingly to his peers. They will gradually become his main partners, but one hopes that the teacher will carry on conversing with all her children, and that she will spend as much time on this as she can.

Before we leave conversation, it would be fitting to draw attention to a context that is particularly suitable for peer-level conversation. This is play, and particularly pretend-play and construction-play. Both lend purpose to talk. Both involve children in negotiation. In fact observers will note that the negotiation is sometimes interleaved with the action, including language, and thus we might have two levels of language working at once. There might be, for instance, language in one of the characters of the pretence and at the same time a sort of management or authorial language in which roles are defined or future action specified. When the children switch from play to management, they move from one discourse to another, one might almost say from one world to another, and they do so with great ease and understanding. If one wanted to specify some language activity that would promise the greatest returns to its participants, this is what one might prescribe.

Long utterances

Long utterances may or may not occur within conversations. The characteristic of a long utterance is that it is made up of several shorter utterances that are joined in some way. When long utterances occur in 'pure' monologue, as when children tell or retell stories, or within conversations (Mark's contribution quoted above was an example of this), we move from situations in which abbreviated 'sentences' are possible. Such a form would be possible in

Where are you going?
To school.

because both participants in the conversation conspire together to make a whole that signals meanings to both. With long utterances, the speaker is on his own. Though he may receive feedback (from the listener's eyes, face, or demeanour, for example) it is not of the ongoing verbal sort that may be built into a conversation.

There is a dearth of cues and prompts. The speaker is left to his own devices. He now has to deal rather differently with problems of coherence, of thematic development, of the orderly presentation of content, as well as with the problems of cohesion to make the language hold together. In short, the speaker is meeting exactly those problems that he will have to face as a writer. More will be said about coherence and cohesion in Chapter 6; for the moment, let us say that long utterances exercise language skills that are valuable in their own right as well as preparing the young child for his future role as a writer.

Spoken language in the later primary years

The first thing to say about spoken language in the later primary years is that the aim to achieve communicative competence remains. So do the goals of using language for diverse purposes, of engaging in mutualised conversations and of making long utterances.

Nevertheless, there are differences between the later and the earlier primary years. Some of these centre upon the use that is made of play. As children get older, the amount of pretend-play diminishes and with it the opportunity for much valuble language-learning. Dramatic play, on the other hand, becomes more formalised, though not necessarily scripted. It still affords many obvious chances of making up language in the guise of being someone different from oneself and of pursuing conversations in that role. Again, it is difficult to imagine many activities that are more profitable from the linguistic point of view — and, of course, the benefits that drama brings do not end with the linguistic but flow over into the emotional, the social, the intellectual, and the attitudinal.

As children grow more proficient in speaking and listening, they become more valuable as partners in conversation and there are abundant opportunities for them to exercise and add to their skills. The reading and writing programmes, as we shall see, should themselves offer many such chances. Topic work allows many more, including collaborative planning and negotiation of a kind different from that conducted before.

Also in the later junior years, group discussions become increasingly possible, without the teacher necessarily being a member of the group. Again, there are examples of this both in Chapter 5 which deals with reading, and in Chapter 7 which looks at group discussion from the point of view of the role of language in learning.

Among the most remarkable evidence of advance will be in what we called 'long utterances'. Children in the top primary will show considerable ability in speaking to the whole class, provided that certain conditions are met. These are: first, that there should have been a lively tradition of using spoken language throughout the primary school; second, that there should have been plenty of previous practice in making long utterances, for example in retelling stories; third, the child needs to have something to say finally, he must feel that his listeners will be interested in what he has to say.

In concluding this chapter, I should like to draw attention to a famous teacher in the old West Riding of Yorkshire named Mrs Pyrah who excelled in getting her children to give talks to their fellows. There was a daily routine in which time was allocated for the purpose. Each day, two or three children would take their turn to talk to the whole class. They were expected to talk for a few minutes each. They could pick their own topic by agreement with the teacher. Usually it would be about some exciting or interesting aspect of their work in school (both Mrs Pyrah and her children were keen naturalists), or perhaps about a book they had read, or about a visit or an excursion they had been on with their parents. This was a class where there was a buoyant atmosphere, where children, their knowledge and their contributions were valued and where a tradition of using language in this way had been established.

The results were remarkable. Moreover, they went far beyond gains in language competence for the work was reflected in higher scores in intelligence tests — to the puzzlement of certain psychologists. It seems that if we want to become intelligent we should behave intelligently. The language programme in this school certainly offered its children the chance to become intelligent.

It is probably safe to make two summarising points to draw the moral from this and from what has been said earlier. First, we must guard against underestimating the extent to which children can develop their language use; and second, when such development takes place, there are emotional, social and intellectual gains which give it significance far beyond the linguistic.

Note

*This is Maureen Shield's useful concept.

4

The Transition to Literacy

Literacy, the business of reading and writing, is built on foundations that need to be securely established well before the child's first
encounters with print. When they are secure, the child is likely to
find that learning to read and write, though each is a complex skill,
is nevertheless a straightforward matter. On the other hand, when
the foundations have not been well laid, the child is likely to
experience great difficulty, and subsequent remedial action is
unlikely to be very effective.

Fundamentally, there is a great deal in common between listening and speaking on the one hand and reading and writing on the
other. All four processes are concerned with meaning — speaking
and writing with putting meaning into language signals, listening
and reading with construing meaning from such signals. Reading
and writing are continuous with earlier language learning in that
both greatly depend in their early stages on language as it has been
learned in the spoken mode. They draw on knowledge of grammar
and lexis that has long been established. This prior knowledge is
one of the child's greatest assets when he turns to master literacy.
Another asset is his previously acquired knowledge of the world.
He now has to employ these sorts of knowledge to deal with the
meanings in the written mode. This is the essential continuity
between earlier language learning and learning to read and write.

But if there is this continuity, there is also discontinuity. It is
not simply that the child will have to learn some new matters —
for that is obvious. The discontinuity comes from his need to
unlearn, or to learn to do without, certain language resources that
have long been second nature to him. In essence, he has to do
without the sound systems of the spoken mode. In addition, he has
to learn that the written mode has somewhat different ways of

employing its grammar and lexis, partly because it has no sound component to exploit and partly because of the different circumstances in which it is proper to use it. Some of these differences, it will be recalled, were explored in Chapter 2.

Earlier in Chapter 2 on spoken language, it was pointed out that the child's proficiency in speaking grows out of his earlier attempts to communicate by using sounds. Sounds to communicate are well developed before the coming of language itself. Then comes the extended process in which the child learns to cope with the conventional sounds of language in order to make and receive and process signals of meaning. The transition is a long one and at all stages sound is important not just as the vehicle for words and grammar, but in its own right in its constitution into significant intonation patterns, to be delivered with variations of pace, voice-colour and volume. Intonation eventually combines with lexis and grammar but for much of the time it is the dominant component. That is why it seems to become second nature to the child. The written mode, in contrast, has no sound at all. Of course, what is written down can always be 'read aloud', and what is spoken can, in a sense, be 'written down,' but sound is not an intrinsic part of the written mode.

From the point of view of the teacher, the problem is how to help the child to do without the sound component. In principle, the answer is simple. It is that sound can be used during the transition stage to literacy, the better to dispense with it later.

What is here called the 'transition stage' or 'transitional reading' is best understood from the perspective of meaning. The true end of reading is to get meaning, by which is meant the construing of meaning from written signals. In the transition stage this process is reversed. Meaning comes first. At first, the paradox may sound startling, but its use merely acknowledges practices that are widely accepted in our schools. In fact, the child's hold on the complexities of reading and writing is simplified when he keeps a tight hold on meaning.

Consider some of these complexities. Take the use of space as an example. Envisage a page with a picture on it of the kind that might be found in an early reading book. There is space at the top of the page and space at the bottom, space between picture and text, space before a line, after a line, between lines, within lines both between letters and between words, space between sentences and, if there are paragraphs, space between them too. Speech, to which the child is well used has, in contrast, no space. It does have pauses, but these do not necessarily coincide either with spaces or with the placing of the new-fangled punctuation marks. When we speak, we frequently run one word into the next so that there is no interval between them. It is not too easy for the literate among us to imagine how this works, for when we become used to printed language we tend to lose our innocence and to think that it is 'natural' for there to be spaces and therefore pauses between all words. When the child is learning to cope with print he has to learn or to be reminded that there are indeed words and that they are in principle separable from each other and that there can be a one-to-one relationship between words spoken and words written down. The child who still thinks that 'meatantaterpie' is one word will certainly have some problems with reading. If this is an isolated misunderstanding, then it is of no great consequence, but if it is only one example of a more generalised kind of misconception then one of the basic understandings that are absolutely necessary as pre-requisites for reading and writing is missing. Hopefully, though, the child will have learned about words before he comes to school.

He must not only understand the independent status of words, he must come to realise that writing also uses other systems and arrangements, such as the use of space to which we referred, that are unknown to speech. Not all these systems need to be mastered at once, but their presence should be noted, and when the child comes to write, the teacher will have to decide when to act and what action to take. An example is punctuation. Most teachers find it profitable to supply and to encourage the child to copy such sentence markers as the capital letter and the full stop from quite early in his career as a writer. As they do so, they begin a long process aim-ed at the eventual mastery of the whole of punctuation.

Spelling is another system, or collection of systems, which belongs exclusively to the written mode and is unknown to speech. We shall consider it further in Chapter 6 which deals with the development of writing. Here, it is enough to say that the child's inability to spell should always cause concern to the teacher. There can be no written composition without spelling and it is important that the teacher should find some ways to ensure that the development of compositional ability is not held up by spelling problems. Apart from getting the child to learn to spell, common ways of coping are for the teacher to supply words on request and for her to organise repositories of words in convenient places and to encourage the child to use them. Lists of days of the week, months of the year, the names of children in the class are commonly made. So are such repositories as pictures with words used to label their 'contents.

The characteristics of transitional reading

The point about transitional reading is that it is not really reading at all, though it can merge imperceptibly into true reading. All reading draws upon previous knowledge and particularly upon established knowledge of language. It is characteristic of transitional reading that it depends on prior success in learning to speak and to listen. It shares this with true reading. What is different about transitional reading is that the child may 'write' his own text. The course of events is like this: he puts meaning into spoken language. This is then written down — usually by the teacher. The child then 'reads' this written version. Of course, he is not so much arriving at meaning as remembering what the original meaning was that he himself had put into speech. As he 'reads' aloud, he will again put this meaning into speech. The process can best be seen in contrast with that of true reading and Figs 4.1 and 4.2 show the difference.

There is, of course, little new in practice here. One of the major ploys of most infant teachers has been to get the child to say something, maybe orally to compose a caption for a picture. The teacher then puts this into the written mode and the child 'reads' it by saying again what he said originally.

Within transitional reading there are various grades of difficulty. Going through them takes the child further in the direction of true reading. Sometimes it will be difficult for an observer to say whether a child is truly reading or is still transitional. It is likely that some encounters with print may be true reading while others are transitional. Some of the ways in which progress can be made are:

(1) leaving a greater interval of time between the writing and the 'reading'. The longer the interval, the more difficult it is for the child to rely on mere memory. Sometimes the interval can be lengthened by going back later to read what has earlier been 'read' transitionally. Part of the game, though, as far as the teacher is concerned, is to ensure success in whatever the child attempts so that he is never frustrated by being asked to do anything which is at that moment too difficult;

(2) having the child compose (orally) more language. Generally, the shorter the piece, the easier for him to cope;

Fig. 4.1: Transitional 'reading': the child begins and ends with meaning

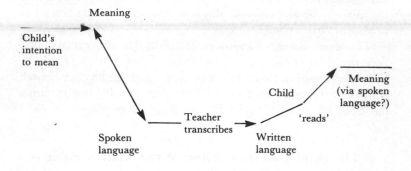

Fig. 4.2: True reading: the reader arrives at meaning at the end of the process

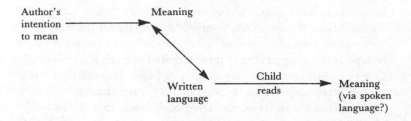

(3)   training the child in the use of the 'Breakthrough to Literacy' materials which will give him a measure of independence of the teacher, for it enables him to find the written form of language without himself being able to spell or to handwrite. 'Breakthrough' brings relative, not complete, independence, and clearly increases the burden on the child. My personal judgement is that it is excellent when it is used properly and that it should be found universally in all infant schools. It sometimes has startlingly good effects on the ability of the child to compose written language while he is still really only on the verge of literacy;

(4)   reading, perhaps collaboratively, what other children at a similar stage of development have written;

(5)   reading other material which is already 'known', such as poems, nursery rhymes, short stories and so on.

The transitional stage can be extended on the principle of

'meaning before reading' so that it overlaps true reading. Such approaches as those above can be the mainstay at one period of the infant's life and can still play a part when the child is a fairly proficient 'true' reader.

This development is shown in Fig. 4.2. The difference is that here the child encounters in the written form something that he knows very well in its spoken form but which he has not himself composed. Once again the child's problem of achieving meaning has been solved even before the 'reading' takes place.

The child's understanding of the written mode and of reading

Before the transition stage can be developed, the child needs to learn a good deal about the nature of the written mode. For instance, he needs to understand about books. He can begin very early. Round about the time he is weaned he is ready for his first book, although in view of his potential for destruction, a rag book might be best at this stage. He may then happily brandish it, occasionally look at it, and sometimes try to turn its page. He is likely to treat it with scant respect, but at least he will learn that there is such a thing, that it can be manipulated and, later, that it can be the object of his and someone else's joint attention. Eventually, he will need to know how books work: that they have pages and that these can be turned over; that there is a 'right' order in which to look at them and a 'right' way to hold them up; and that they are somehow connected with stories and have interesting pictures.

Before he can begin to read, it is essential that his knowledge of print should go further than this. In particular, he needs to know the crucial directionality rule — that print goes from left to right and that each consecutive line is arranged under its predecessor. This spatial organisation replaces the serial organisation in time which is characteristic of the spoken language. Here we have one of those 'simple' truths that become obvious when they are known but which can cause immense confusion if they are not understood.

A further essential understanding is that of the difference between telling and reading. This understanding is at a purely practical level — to the effect that there is a difference between the two; and that although one can tell a story from a book, reading that story entails doing something quite different. Closely allied to this is the notion that there is a one-to-one correspondence between the word as written down and the word as uttered when there is reading aloud. Several researchers have found what has been called 'cognitive confusion' in the minds of children at the time when they are beginning to learn to read. The child from an educated home is likely to have the advantage here. He is likely already to know about print and about books and how they are arranged. He is likely, too, to understand this crucial difference between reading and telling. His knowledge will have been formed over literally years of encounters with books, print and with story-reading and story-telling. Schools need to take decisive action when such knowledge is not well-formed in a child. In this, as in so many other matters, they can take a leaf out of the parents' book and do, slightly more pointedly and more quickly, what the parents have been doing over a longer period of time. Again, there may be need also to support those parents who have not succeeded in this respect, perhaps because they did not understand what they ought to have done or how they should have done it.

The point of all this, of course, is that much education concerning both the written mode itself and the nature of reading needs to go on before the child enters into transitional reading. There is, however, more to it than we have yet indicated. It is very difficult to think of anything that will have more beneficial results than reading to the child during his preschool years. The process should begin as early as possible. We shall come back shortly to the notion of a continuing programme of spoken language going on side-by-side with reading and writing, but there can be no doubt that one of the best ways of fostering spoken language and at the same time tightening the bonds between children and their parents is in handling books, discussing their content, looking forward to them, and backward too to recall them later, pointing out words and interesting bits of pictures. Such activities have great value both intellectually and in the formation of attitudes. It is vital, of course, both to initial reading and to its long-term development that these should be positive attitudes and that the child should look forward to his encounters with print with great pleasure.

Reading aloud to children has other values, some of which will be further explored in Chapter 5 which is concerned with the development of reading. Written (including, of course, printed) language differs in significant ways from spoken language. It is necessary for the child to build up his knowledge of such language so that he can process it for meaning. It is possible to delay this until he can take such language in for himself through his eye. But consider the advantage of the child who has been able to take in such language aurally. Think of what such a child will know and understand if he has had a story each day between the ages of 2 and 5. He will go to school with a thousand stories, and all that he has learned from them, under his belt. He will know how print works; he will know a good deal about how literary language works; he will know something of how authors work, too. His task as a budding reader will be immensely easier than that of the child who knows little of such matters.

We said earlier that reading draws on knowledge of spoken language. It is vital that the development of spoken language should go on side-by-side with transitional reading and writing. Spoken language, as it extends both in content and in use, will go on nourishing the child's ability to read and write. Increasingly, too, reading and writing will influence and nourish his ability to speak and listen.

Non-systematic encounters with print

The teacher deals somewhat systematically with reading and writing, helping the child to progress from stage to stage There is another important side to the child's experience and it comes when he meets print more or less randomly in his daily life in the environment that surrounds him. This side of his experience is also important. He meets words and stretches of language on posters, outside shops, on notices, on the television, on letters that come into his house, in newspapers, on packets of food at the breakfast table. Most of these encounters are outside school. Many of them are experienced before he becomes a schoolboy. Some homes and some parents handle their opportunities superbly, encouraging the child's interest and feeding him enough, and not too much, relevant information. Other homes and parents, alas, ignore their chances and theirs are the children who may not become so sensitive to print.

What happens when these encounters are most effective is invaluable and is, perhaps, surprising in its sophistication. For it becomes apparent that the child begins to use a variety of contextual clues to manage his 'understanding' of print even before he can read. Thus he expects certain words to appear at the beginning or end of television programmes or during television advertising displays. If he is interested in motor cars, he expects to see the name appear on the bonnet or the boot. He distinguishes 'Corn Flakes' from the designs and non-linguistic marks on the package and also from other stretches of language. Already, he begins to understand that language and context and situation are closely related and that each can be used to identify and explain the other. Whether at this stage the child is actually reading or not seems to matter very little. Developmentally, he is on his way, already gaining fundamental insights.

Giving the child practical help: handwriting and layout skills

Handwriting needs to be distinguished very positively from composition, which we shall call 'writing' henceforth. Each makes different sorts of demand on the child and he needs different sorts of help in order to cope. Some children are taught handwriting at home before they enrol at school. Home teaching may not entail teaching the particular script that the school would want the child to learn. Often it takes its cues from alphabet books and teaches the child upper-case letters, so that he comes to school writing only capitals. Further, it is unusual for parents to offer systematic help on layout skills — on what we might think of as the use of space, or as arrangement on the page. None of this disables the child. Of course, it might possibly have been better if he had not learned only to handwrite upper case letters, better still if he had been taught the school's script. But as a rule he is likely to accept that at school he must learn the school's way and will try very hard to do so, though there may be some 'interference' from his old learning.

In what follows we shall assume that the child is beginning to learn. The eventual aim, of course, is to have him write automatically. Now, 'automatically' does not mean that he should handwrite like an automaton. It means that he will be able to handwrite with minimal attention to his letter shapes, joins, positions on the line, spacing, and so on. When handwriting is automatic in this way, it gives the handwriter an option that he would not otherwise have, for he can now consciously decide to pay attention to what he is doing, to take greater care, perhaps even to make some of his letters differently. In short, it will always be possible for him to override his automatic habits, just as a car driver can choose to pay attention to the way in which he changes gear or manipulates other controls in the vehicle. But just as the driver can stay 'automatic' and thus free himself to deal with any novel hazards that present themselves, so the handwriter can choose to give his attention to writing rather than to handwriting. What the teacher has to do is to institute a train of events that will give the child this option.

Handwriting is a psychomotor skill or, if you prefer, a complex of psychomotor skills which have to be brought together or 'orchestrated'. When we think of skills we know that there are some matters that are crucial. There must be practice. Skills do not simply appear ready-formed. And there must be feedback. The teacher's task, then, is to institute practice and to give some of this feedback herself. There is, of course, a prior question. It is: practise what, exactly? This brings us to a matter which needs to be decided by the staff as a whole, especially if they deal with infants. It is to determine which script, out of several possibilities, is to be adopted as standard. In the interests of continuity and progression, it is clearly advisable that there should be standardisation.

What follows is not an attempt to advise on the merits of any particular script; it applies to all scripts. Once a script has been decided upon, it becomes the target. It also constitutes a series of models that the child must practise. These models are of two sorts, shape and process. Both provide examples that the child can copy. Success in following the 'shape' model will result in the child reproducing a shape like that of his model. Success in process will mean that the child not only produces the desired letter shape but that he does it in a prescribed way.

The provision of models is the teacher's job. We shall shortly discuss how these models may be supplied and also the precise use that the child may make of them. A process of development is involved and it includes a seeming paradox, for the purpose of these models is eventually to be able to do without them.

This anticipates a great part of the developmental process, for there are other stages to be gone through before handwriting is even attempted. Handwriting is essentially making marks upon a surface. The marks are highly conventionalised but before the child can tackle conventional marks, he must have plenty of experience in making other sorts of marks. Handwriting utilises prior experience in using different kinds of instruments — not only pencils and ballpoints, but fibretips, crayons, chalk, paint brushes and the fingers themselves. Surfaces differ in texture, colour, size and shape. Experience in using a variety of surfaces and of marking instruments and materials will stand the child in good stead. His task is to develop the fine muscle control and coordination between hand and arm and eye that will be needed for handwriting.

Motivation is not usually lacking. Sometimes his parents will have taught him because he importuned. Often he will have begun to 'write' before he gets to school and his writing will have taken certain forms. At this stage he will probably not distinguish clearly between handwriting and composition and so we get what Marie Clay has described in her book *What Did I Write?* as the recurring and flexibility principles. In true course of 'writing' the child spontaneously repeats certain forms (the recurring principle) and also varies certain forms (the flexibility principle). As yet there is no necessary connection with any truly alphabetic letters. The process is reminiscent of babbling, and presumably has similar development value.

How the teacher organises the teaching and learning of handwriting is a matter for her judgement. It may be in class sessions, group sessions, individual sessions, more formally in sustained periods or less formally in opportunistic encounters. However, the broad track that the child must follow is quite clear. He moves from 'drawing' an example of a letter, of a model provided by the teacher, through various stages of mastery. It is important that the model should be a good one. Observations in many classrooms show that this is not always the case. The model should always be carefully wrought by the teacher. It will, as we said, have two aspects — the product and the process. The product will be left on the page for the child to use. It should be the 'right' height and width for its purpose. The spacing should be 'right' also, particularly when several letters are being copied. This means that the teacher should use a writing instrument of the same kind as the child is using. If the teacher uses a broad felt-tip and the child copies in pencil, the spacing and possibly the sizes of the letters she makes are likely to be unsuitable for him. In other words, if the child copies in fine point letters that have been done more thickly, he will either get his spacing wrong or, if he follows the teacher's, will end with spacing that looks odd.

Copying can be underneath, or be superimposed upon, or be written above the model provided. Progression is involved here with superimposition being the elementary stage, sometimes done as tracing on tracing paper. Copying underneath is easier than copying above because the model is before the eye as the copying is done. When copying is done above the model, this is not always so.

Generally, at this stage, though, the model is in front of the child. As he compares his product with that before him, he can make adjustments. Thus he takes feedback as he compares his own effort with the model. Taking feedback, however, is itself a skilled job and he may need help. He may have to be shown that, in some respects that are important, he is not following the model accurately. He may need to be reminded of the process model. The point is, of course, that at this stage he is working with two models, one on the page and the other, the process model, in his mind. His knowledge of the latter may have to be refreshed from time to time. It follows from this that if the teacher is to give the right sort of feedback, she must be involved in the action. Giving feedback on process may be the result of what she deduces from the child's product. On the other hand, if she is observing what the child actually does, she can give any necessary corrective feedback with more certainty. This brings us to another important point about feedback. If it is to be effective, there needs to be as short a time as possible between the child's action and his consideration of feedback. The next step, which again should be tackled as soon as possible, is to incorporate what has been learned from the feedback into further practice. Finally, we should remember that feedback ought to be confirmatory as well as corrective, for the child needs to know what he is doing right quite as much as he needs to know what he is doing wrong.

The broad process, then, is that the child learns from process and product models. As he does so, his perception and understanding of these models is increased. The job of the teacher is in first providing the models, then in explaining them as time goes on. This makes it possible for the child to get increasingly valuable feedback for himself from his own efforts. In the meantime, the teacher herself must give feedback directly.

As this goes on, the location of the model changes. The process model is ephemeral and has needed to be memorised from the start. It becomes more vivid and more clearly sequential as time goes on. The product model, however, graduallly transfers itself from the page to the mind, so that the child's comparisons are with an image that has now become permanent in the mind, rather than with marks on the paper. Of the two, the process model is, in any case, probably the more important.

The child moves from the three sorts of copying noted above — which all have the result of leaving two sorts of handwriting on the page, the teacher's and the child's — to more remote sorts of copying. At this point learning to handwrite becomes enmeshed with the business of coping with spelling. Personal word books, in which the teacher writes words that the child has requested, serve the primary purpose of providing spellings and the secondary purpose of providing model handwriting. The same is true of sentence books in which the teacher writes sentences that the child has composed orally, so that the child may copy them out. In these ways the models become more remote. They move from the short-term and into the long-term memory.

The provision of models and feedback is only part of the story, however, for the child is faced with other problems. The first is: exactly where on the page should the handwriting be done? This only emerges when the child has moved beyond the first phase of copying on or below, or above the teacher's model. Many teachers offer help by marking with a dot the exact place where the child should begin to write. Some also offer help with right-hand-side margins.

Spacing between lines is another problem which comes with the later stages of copying. Often, controversy arises in the school about the use of lined paper. Some feel that lines give the child valuable guidance. Others insist that lines are altogether too confining and that, far from helping they actually impose undue worries on the child. One school that I know solves this problem in a very successful way. The children use lined paper for some of the time but not for all. A further helpful arrangement by the same school recognises that the size of letters changes as the children develop and that therefore the space between the lines ought to change also. They use ruled lines done in bold felt-tip on a guide sheet which the children are taught to place underneath, and to square up with, the sheet on which they write. It works exactly the same as do the guide lines that are sometimes supplied with writing pads for adults. There seem to be two advantages in using them. First, the lines do not appear on the finished product — which gives it a clean and uncluttered look. Second, the child is able to progress from one guide sheet to another, and as he progresses the spacing between the lines is reduced. This school also has children who have progressed into working without guide lines of any sort. The results seem to have been most successful.

The teacher needs to give her attention to other matters which are attendant upon the handwriting process. Children need guidance on how to grip their writing tool, on how and where to sit in relation to the table, how to position their paper in relation to the table and to themselves, what angle to keep the paper at, whether to move the paper during the writing of a line, and so on.

It seems to be established that the position that gives most control is one where the head is some distance from the paper (that is, when the back is moderately straight), when the writer leans neither to left nor to right, and when the point of contact between pencil and paper is equidistant from each eye. However, when one looks at adults, including teachers, writing, one sees that they adopt postures of all kinds and rarely write with the paper square in front of them. Perhaps the moral should be to encourage children to find a posture that is comfortable to them. Handicapped children and left-handers (who are also handicapped in terms of the English writing system, which seems to have been designed for right-handers) need to make their own special arrangements.

Giving the child practical help: choosing reading matter for beginners

When the question is raised: who is the best author for children who are at the beginning of the transitional stage? there can be no doubt about the answer. The only suitable author is the child himself. This is because of the nature of transitional reading. The process behind the production of the text is one which depends on the child's ability to compose oral language. It is then that language that is put into written form. Whether it is the teacher who acts as a scribe or the child who finds the written forms for himself, for example by using Breakthrough to Literacy materials, the original source is the child himself. The transitional stage runs through processes which involve the child in tasks which get steadily harder and which move towards true reading. The amount that the child composes is increased. The interval of time between composing and 'reading back' is lengthened. The gradations are introduced not to perplex the child but to give him chances to rely less and less on the memory of his own composition and more on processing the visual signals left on the page.

A second stage comes when the reading matter is not composed by the child but is a written representation of what he already knows.

A third stage operating the same principle may take the child well into the realm of true reading. In such cases the 'meaning first' approach boosts the child's power to tackle a range of texts that would otherwise be beyond him. Examples of this are:

(1)   when he rereads a story that has already been read to him;

(2)   when he reads a different version (perhaps a shorter one) of
      a story that has been read to him;
(3)   when the teacher, in person or on tape, reads and the child
      follows.

In such ways the transition from oracy to initial literacy and
beyond is managed. The characteristic feature of both transitional
reading and its continuation beyond the point of true reading is
its use of a spoken form of language which has the potential either
of registering meaning (if it is the child's own language) or of conveying meaning (if it is someone else's language). The feature of
language with which the child is most familiar is thus employed
to ease his way into literacy. Spoken language is the bridge — and
it can be extended as long, and as far, as the teacher judges.
Generally speaking, though, from now on the two modes of
language gradually grow less intimate in their connections.

As yet, it will be noted, no commercial reading texts have made
their appearance. Neither have so-called prereaders. We shall turn
to a discussion of their characteristics in Chapter 5.

5

The Development of Reading

This is a long chapter and it might be as well to indicate both how its contents are arranged and how it relates to other chapters.

Chapter 4 stressed the importance of the transition stage in literacy. Its characteristics were that: the spoken and written modes of language were, in effect, unified; the child at that stage did not engage in true reading but began with meaning, engaging in what might be called 'cross-moding' — fitting the text to the meaning; the child did not engage, either, in true writing but was supplied with a written form for what he composed orally. These activities gradually move towards true reading and writing and, as they do, the child also learns the skills of handwriting and layout and, in a very rudimentary form, of spelling as well. Parallel with this were the child's informal, but invaluable, encounters with print in his environment and from listening as stories were read to him. The antecedents of the transitional stage lie in spoken language and in an increasing knowledge of the world. After the transitional stage, not only do true reading and writing emerge; they also grow apart from each other, though without ever losing their ability strongly to influence each other.

This chapter deals with the further development of reading ability. Its method is to present and to argue the case for the elements of a reading programme which is seen as a constituent part of the fuller language policy. As each element is described, some of the most important parts of the processes of reading and learning to read are discussed. Thus, along with element (3), which argues that the child should read mainly books that he has himself chosen, a critique of commercial reading schemes is developed, including an analysis of 'whole word' and 'phonic' methods. Element (4), which deals with how the teacher can help the child, attends to such diverse matters as the reading environment, which itself includes the furnishing and layout of the classroom, and, more specifically, with the use of the reading conference and approaches such as group techniques that the teacher can employ. Element (5), which deals with the use of language to learn, is a natural development of a major theme of the book, which has been concerned throughout with the relationship of language to learning. This theme, including the role of reading, is dealt with in Chapter 7.

The five elements of the reading programme are:

(1) reading the work of classroom authors (in other words, reading matter written within the school);
(2) the teacher reading aloud to the children;
(3) the children reading freely chosen books;
(4) reading instruction: the help given by the teacher;
(5) the children using language to learn.

Element (1): reading classroom authors

If what was said when we dealt with the transition stage to literacy is true, the children will accept that it is normal and expected that they should write in order that what they have written might be read. It was stressed that the best reading matter, leaving aside what he comes across in his more casual encounters with print, is the child's own language. Not only will he start with meaning; he will also, by definition, be familiar with the grammar and lexis; the level of formality at which the language is pitched will suit him; and both the range of content and the level of conceptual understanding will have been set by him. In reading there should always be a match of some sort between the child's language and the language of the text. In this case we have an identity.

Initially, the teacher will act as scribe, for the child's attempts at handwriting will not yet be adequate to the task. Later still, he will acquire a measure of independence in actually writing down what he has previously 'said'. At all these stages he will read back what he has composed. This is the essence of transitional reading — that he starts with meaning. It was suggested that three variants might be introduced to help with the gradual progression into true reading. The first was that from time to time the interval between composing and reading back might be increased. The object of this exercise, of course, is not to defeat or to frustrate the child but to give him as easy a chance as possible of slipping into real reading. The second variant was that, in collaboration with other children, he might begin to read what they have written. One justification for this has as much to do with the development of writing as with the development of reading. Such activity presents the writer with a rare opportunity to receive feedback and therefore to learn to compose his writing with the needs of the reader in mind. It is a slow job, but there is no doubt that the budding writer can now begin to learn this principle that his writing is for other people. The third variant was that he ought to 'read' texts that he had met in some way before, but which he had not himself written.

Other visible classroom authors include the teacher. There is no doubt that she can fit a book to the interests, language, needs and abilities of a child better than any commercial author who has to write for a mass audience. It is, too, a valuable lesson for the reader to learn that in principle all pieces of writing actually do have an author, and that the author is trying to communicate with whoever reads his work. This is particularly necessary as much of the print encountered casually in the environment, for example at the breakfast table, is anonymous to the extent of appearing to have no author at all.

Element (2): the teacher reading aloud

This element involves the teacher reading regularly to children — and by 'regularly' is meant 'at least once daily throughout the primary years'.

The practice of reading aloud is almost universal as a daily occurrence in nursery and infant classes but seems to tail off as children get older. There is much to be said for continuing the practice — even into the secondary years and beyond into further and higher education.

There are several reasons for advocating such an element in the reading programme. For instance, it extends the children's range of interests. Most of us on looking back to our own childhood will recall that listening to something being read sparked off an enduring interest in a certain author, or in a type of story or poem, or in a particular setting or subject matter.

Written material which would otherwise be inaccessible to children becomes available when it is read to them because the person who is reading aloud has already done part of the work in getting to the meaning. It is a way of cross-moding, of introducing

72

intonation patterns and voice qualities into the business of understanding. Thus the child's developed listening skills are used instead of his reading skills. This alone would be enough to justify a sustained programme of reading aloud to children. But, of course, much more happens. The child is led into meaningful encounters with new words, new grammatical forms, new styles of expression. He can then use these as basic material on which to draw for his own reading and writing. Further, the programme will take him into new genres and make him more familiar with the way they work. He will encounter short stories and longer stories, articles, humorous writings, poems and other verse, letters, and so on, gaining a practical knowledge which will surely stand him in good stead later in his own career as reader and writer.

In order to make a choice of materials, the teacher will need a wide and increasing knowledge of what is available. In making her choices, there is one fact that must be very comforting to her, for the beauty of reading aloud is that it is quite possible for children who are of different levels of ability each to gain from what is being offered. In this way, reading aloud is unlike many other activities where learning, being stictly sequential or hierarchical, can be mapped out in advance. A multiplicity of things can be gained from listening to a text being read aloud. Another way of putting it is that effective writing can work at different levels. One child might be interested in factual subject matter, another in background, whilst a third might be carried along by the sheer excitement of the tale or through his identification with a character. One does not need to understand everything in order to gain something.

For such reasons, it would be a mistake to restrict the programme to fiction. Poetry, songs, lyrics, jokes, news items and letters all should find a place. There is one great proviso: the programme will only succeed if the children remain interested. Here, perhaps, a word of warning and of comfort is called for. It would be a mistake to suppose that all readings will generate the same level of interest or that all chldren will be equally interested all the time. The wise teacher will be looking for certain signs — of enthusiasm when reading aloud is imminent, rapt attention while it is in progress, expressions of satisfaction and requests for repeats afterwards. These show that the teacher is hitting the jackpot. It does not matter if she cannot do this all the time, but she should be able to do it for much of the time.

If there is a persistent lack of success, it may be due to several factors. Poor reading aloud may be one of them. In the privacy

73

and intimacy of story reading the teacher can afford to lose some of her inhibitions and be prepared to 'act out' characters, to experiment with voices, to use pauses dramatically, to go for larger intonation contours, to vary the dynamics and generally to speak up and to use her eyes to 'take in' all the members of her group. She must also plan matters so that there are likely to be few interruptions, whether from noise, messengers and visitors from outside, or from children inside. Occasional inattentiveness and minor misbehaviours can be ignored in order to let the reading make an impact. By her demeanour and by what she says about the activity, the teacher should let it be known that it carries her highest priority. Her expectations of the ways in which her children should behave should thus become very compelling.

She should not forget that the venture is indeed a partnership. The children's goodwill is vital. Accordingly, she might let it be known that she will always consider their suggestions for reading aloud — certainly to the extent of discussing them, and thanking the children whether or not their suggestions are taken up.

The choice of reading matter will always remain somewhat hazardous. There will always be an element of risk, for no-one can predict outcomes with certainty. Attitudes, as always, are in the making and it is important that the teacher should reveal that she, too, does not like everything that is written: that there are some bad poems, stories, articles, and so on and, further, that she expects tastes to differ so that even if a story is a good one, not everybody will necessarily enjoy it. She should collect reactions from the children, first because she values them and then she should explain that she wants all the help she can get in making her future choices. Finally, she should let it be known that if, during the course of her reading, it becomes obvious to her or to her class that a mistake has been made, she will bring her reading to a tidy close and offer something else instead.

This theme of consulting children and discussing her readings with them is valuable well beyond the confines of the reading programme. Getting children to express their likes and dislikes is good in itself. Getting them to give reasons for their preferences is much better. When this happens a major breakthrough occurs, for at such times the child is making a significant advance, both in his knowledge and in the use that he makes of that knowledge. In effect, he is being invited to select or to form, and then to use, criteria, to apply them in practice and to report on his findings. It is in such activities that the basis for future enjoyment is being laid, as is the foundation for the child's career as a discerning reader.

There is more to be said about choice. As we pointed out earlier, the field is so wide that the teacher will need a good deal of help if she is to make the most of her chances. As well as enlisting the aid of her children, she will need the cooperation of her colleagues both inside and outside the school. One way in which this can be achieved is through an arrangement for reviewing books and other materials from the point of view of their suitability and usefulness in school. Some colleagues might be asked to keep an eye on new fiction, others, according to their tastes, on new poetry, others on publishers' lists, so that new editions of older works do not slip by unnoticed. There is much to be said for trading such information with the staff of a neighbouring school. Further help is sometimes organised by the public library system where there may be a range of procedures for involving teachers. In at least one county, the children's librarian organises panels of teachers to review books and then publishes their findings to teachers.

Element (3): the children reading freely chosen books

Giving the child a measure of choice of reading materials (for his private reading) is not a new idea. It often happens as an adjunct to his progress through a reading scheme. What is suggested now is much more radical. It is that a free choice of books should replace the reading scheme altogether. By 'reading scheme' is meant any series of books that is written to provide progressive exercise in reading for children who have not yet reached the stage of fully autonomous reading.

This goes against the grain of existing practice and so it will be necessary to argue a case. Consequently, this section will analyse both whole-word and phonic approaches to reading and will indicate what effect the employment of such approaches is likely to have on the language and style of reading books. Part of the case for a free choice is that existing reading schemes are for the most part inadequate and counterproductive. There is, too, this other aspect of the argument — which is that children need to be encouraged to take responsibility for their own choice of reading matter from as early as possible because they need to build up good attitudes to books and to other printed matter.

Giving children a free choice has important consequences for everyone. For example the teacher's role has to change considerably (this will be discussed in connection with the element (4) of the programme). But it is important to say at the outset that free choice does not mean that the child is offered no help in choosing his books — for the teacher can give much assistance more directly through her overall choice of books (out of which the child makes his own choices), and indirectly through her control of the reading environment.

Before we can go on to discuss this, it is necessary to look more closely at what I call 'word-centred' approaches to reading and to their consequences for the writing of books.

Some characteristics of commercial reading schemes

There are three sorts of reasons why we should want a child to read a book (and why the child himself might want to read it):

(1) literary merit — the appeal of story line, setting, characters, and so on, to the child;
(2) factual interest — the child may want to learn about, or become involved in, a particular subject. This is likely to lead the child into non-fiction but by no means exclusively so;
(3) its worth in increasing the child's reading competence.

While the first and second are powerful enough to stand alone, the third never is. In other words, it is not, in my view, sufficient to buy books which have little or no literary merit or factual interest, simply because the publishers assert that such books will make better readers of our children.

The first two reasons seem self-evident, at least in broad terms, though one could argue about what 'literary merit' is. The third reason demands closer examination. First, it is essential to remind ourselves that reading is always an affective (or orectic) as well as a cognitive matter. It has to do with the processing of information taken into the mind; but it is also a matter of emotion, attitude and volition, both in what the reader brings to the text and in what he takes away from it. Each of the three reasons given above might serve to motivate a particular child, but the third on its own might lead to undesirable results. For example, when a reading scheme is taken as being justified on this third ground, it leads to the competitive and unfounded notion that racing through a reading scheme is what progress in reading is all about. The troubles with such competitiveness are manifold. For instance, in competitions there is really one one winner. Consequently, there grows up, not only in the child, but in some parents as well, a wrong and unhelpful view of the chlid's development.

Books written as mere 'reading fodder' are also unlikely to relate reading to other aspects of the worlds of real life and of make-believe. As an activity, it is pushed into isolation. When this happens, some of the most potent long-term reasons for reading are absent, for it is precisely the literary and information values that form positive attitudes and make the child want to continue to be a reader throughout his life.

The moral of this, of course, is that teachers should only make available books that have real merit — literary or informational, or both. Of course, if such merit could be combined with the property of helping to increase competence, we should be most happy. Unfortunately, the prevailing ideas which underlie the writing of many primers work against this ideal. In some instances they make it quite impossible for a book to have any lasting merit.

Now, the inadequacies that are alleged to be characteristic of reading schemes in general come about for a number of reasons. It is important that the teacher should understand these, for the responsibility of deciding what books will or will not be made available is essentially a professional one.

In the first place, many reading schemes tend to be founded on outmoded notions of what reading is. Not all, it is true, are equally at fault in this respect. Some begin inanely but improve as the series progresses. Most of them suffer from two faults — and these lie in the category by which the books are usually 'justified', which is that they help the child to become a better reader. The two faults are closely linked. They are that the authors, and therefore their books, are word-fixated, and that they actually ignore and may impede the development of some of the most important skills of reading.

Word-fixation and its consequences

Word-fixation is a disease of writers which can be transmitted only too easily to children and, alas, to teachers as well. It stunts children's growth and is so debilitating to adults that it comes close to making them unfit to be in charge of children who are learning to read. There are two strains of the disease, both virulent. One is the whole word approach and the other is phonics. Authors suffering from either believe that reading is basically a matter of coping with words. In the first you simply recognise a word by looking at it; in the second you get to the same place by some sort of analysis and synthesis of what are supposed to be the constituent 'sounds' of the word. There is just enough truth in both beliefs to make them plausible. In the whole word approach the salient method is for the authors to repeat a word sufficiently often for the child to recognise it whenever it is presented again. The phonics authors go for what they think is a certain regularity, using words in which a particular pattern of correspondence between spelling and 'sound' is repeated. The idea is that whenever the child then meets that correspondence in 'new' words he will be able to work out the sound for himself. On the pure phonics method that seems to be all there is to it, except that children also need practice in 'blending' constituent sounds together in 'new' words, but once they are skilled in these procedures, the back of reading is broken — or so it is thought.

Turning first to the whole-word approach, we shall see that the method has certain undesirable outcomes. Materials tend to proliferate spectacularly in order to give adequate repetitions, which may be good for publishers but is not necessarily good for children. One older example which serves to illustrate this tendency is the Happy Venture series which is still in use and which was once among the most widely used of all schemes in British schools. It progressed, somewhat curiously, from an Introductory Book to Book One and then three more books were added to take the series to five. Throughout, there was vocabulary control, with the number of new words on each page tightly rationed, for it was held that it was only when the 'new word burden' was thus minimised that the child would have the chance to remember and so to recognise again the very few new words to appear on each page. Even so, it was soon felt that there was not enough repetition to allow children to cotton on, and so four more books — the so-called Playbooks — were added with an almost identical vocabulary. Still there was not enough repetition and so a series of supplementary 'library' books was added, over 30 of them, again with the same basic vocabulary. And, in case that was not enough, the total scheme was extended to offer flash cards and other non-book materials — again exercising the same basic vocabulary. The sad thing was that this proliferation, though commercially successful, was doomed from the start. It is perfectly true that many children learned to read with the materials — but not because of their rationale, for there is no way that word recognition equals reading, no matter how much repetition there may be. Such success as children had was due mainly to other factors.

Given a controlled vocabulary, whether of sight words or of phonically 'regular' words, it is extremely difficult for an author to write a book which has literary merit. The introduction of new words being strictly limited, that author falls into a double bind. He may or may not have something to say. If he has, the twin needs to repeat words and to avoid new ones take possession of his mind, and the most odd behaviour results. When this behaviour becomes pathological, as it often does, it gives rise to a form of language known as 'primerese' — an aberrant form if ever there was one, and one which is found nowhere outside the pages of early reading books. It is never easy, once an author has contacted the disease, for him to recover fully. Partial remission is sometimes possible and when we look at the later books in a reading scheme we sometimes find that they are not as blighted as the earlier ones. Occasionally, good health in the form of literary skills does reassert itself and we get a tale or a chapter that is worth reading for its own sake. But it takes a considerable author, if he is at all constrained by the necessities of a controlled vocabulary, ever to deliver the literary goods. Many fail. Most do not even try, having reduced their perceptions of their craft so that they see their task as merely that of repeating the same words, or the same phonic patterns, in different sentences.

Phonics control brings rather different problems from those associated with the whole-word approach. Here the hope is to give the child access to words which have similar patterns as those in the prototypes, and to equip him with the 'sounding out' and 'blending' skills that will allow him to tackle (some) previously unmet words without any help from anyone. In practice there are some very considerable obstacles in the way of success.

We read to get meaning. Putting sound into the process, as phonics does, is at best a somewhat extraneous means to an end. At its worst, phonic analysis and synthesis are an encumbrance which slows down the process, sometimes to the extent of causing it to fail. It is known that speed is essential to reading at all stages, because of the limited capacity of the short-term memory. The short-term memory holds information while it is processed. It cannot hold many items and those that it does hold it cannot retain for very long. In so far as 'sounding out' and blending slow down the process, they may overburden the short-term memory and thus make the business of processing for meaning more difficult or even impossible. That is why phonics may be self-defeating. It is only fair to say that there might be a way around this particular limitation. For example, a phonic puzzling-out of the word in a sentence might be followed by a second and quicker run-through of the sentence which would be necessary if meaning is to be achieved.

However, the case against phonics does not rest there. More is involved than the possible distortion of texts and the probable slowing down of the reading process to the point where it is aborted. Even if phonics were to be employed, it is necessary to remember that it does not purport to deal with all the sound elements of language. From the chapter on language, it will be recalled that we are concerned with two basic sorts of sounds — the constituent phonemes and the larger intonation patterns. Phonics is a way of trying to teach the child to deal with the first. It has nothing to say about the second sort. If it is neglected we often get from the child who is 'reading aloud' a very staccato delivery appropriate, perhaps, for reading a list but quite unsuitable for normal sentences. As the tune is intimately connected with meaning, such a delivery makes us doubt whether the process of construing meaning is going on properly.

All of this takes us back to that basic and widespread misunderstanding about reading, which is that it is essentially concerned with words. It is much sounder to think of it as being concerned with *language* and there is more to language than mere words. It follows from this that any approach to reading which limits itself to words alone is likely to be inadequate and this is just as true of whole-word approaches as it is of phonics. The idea behind both seems to be 'Get the words, and the rest will follow.' Sometimes this works, but it is just as likely to let the young reader down. The children who cope are the ones who are the strongest, who know language best, and who are smart enough to make allowances for the deficiencies of the principles by which they are supposed to be learning. What they do, if they are to succeed, is to devise alternative strategies of their own. Thus, many children who are thought to have learned to read by a phonics or by a whole-word approach have learned *in spite of such approaches*. Their strategies may be similar to those that they have employed for years to get meaning from listening to spoken language.

This is not to say that word recognition can play no part in reading. It has a place, in particular at the earliest stages. But we should remember that sometimes reading does not *begin* with the

recognition of words but ends with their *identification* through meaning — by inference so to speak. Leaving this possibility aside —
and it is really only another way of saying that one way to deal
with words is to meet them in context — let us look at the correspondences which the other word-fixated approach (phonics) tries to
explain and which are central in any attempt to justify it as an
approach.

When we deal with these correspondences between letters and
sounds (or between graphemes and phonemes), there are several
points to be made. The first is to insist that letters, either alone
or in combination, never actually 'say' anything. Some children
in the very early stages have had to learn this the hard way; they
actually expect to hear a sound when they look at a letter! However,
let us assume that 'says' and 'sounding out' are being used loosely
or metaphorically. There is a basic problem in English that there
are about 45 sounds and only 26 letters. Sometimes a combination
of letters corresponds to a single sound; sometimes a letter or a combination of letters corresponds to more than one sound. The point
is that there is no simple one-to-one relationship. The child's basic
problem in this respect is to find his way through what must seem
to be a tangle of relationships. The teacher has to be very careful
and must not conclude that this is an easy business. It is easy to
be misled about this because expert readers, as opposed to begin-
ners, have learned to ignore or otherwise cope with the difficulties.
To a beginning or struggling reader, on the other hand, the problem might be fatal, totally beyond his understanding, and the
resulting frustration bad for both his self-image and his attitude to
reading. His thinking may go 'Others can do this. I can't. I must
be thick,' or 'Reading is daft. I don't like it.'

Let us assume that the child picks the right correspondence. He
then has the problem of combining the sound with adjacent sounds.
This problem is inevitable when we try to split up language into
the constituent sounds of its words. One way in which phonics tries
to proceed is by attaching a vowel element to each consonant. Thus
the letter 't' is made to say 'tuh', letter 'b' is supposed to say
'buh', and so on. Even if we allow for the moment that letter 't'
and letter 'b' do actually 'say' something, what they never say under
any circumstances whatever is 'tuh' or 'buh' or anything similar.
Children, therefore, are left to sort out a mess. This they are
sometimes taught to do by 'blending' — the process by which the
teacher tries to have her cake and eat it. For, in order to blend
successfully, the original phonic sounds have to be modified. What

has been learned has to be unlearned, or else it will not work.

It is true that some of these difficulties may be alleviated. If the teacher presents a letter within its environment, in connection with other sounds, she can then leave the deductions about the sounds that that letter makes to the child. Thus, instead of teaching that the letter 'b' says 'buh' (which we know it does not) she can present a list like this:

big
bin
bit
ban
bat

and so on. This makes a bad job less bad. If this path is chosen, it is best, in my view, to concentrate on letters that are in initial position because this avoids other nasty difficulties and also because initial clues are most valuable to the reader.

But the difficulties with phonics are intrinsic to language itself. We have noted that a vocalic intrusion occurs whenever we try to isolate a consonant. There are other complications. Sounds, as we have pointed out, always appear in an environment of other sounds, and to some extent it is this environment that determines the sound. Thus the sound of a word is not fixed as the simple addition of the first sound plus the second sound, plus the third sound, and so on until we have combined all the constituents. Instead there is a complex interaction in which one sound affects the way in which another sound is uttered. Similar influences operate between words as well as within words. In short, the environment is made up of larger stretches of language. Its effects are particularly striking with vowels. For example, we might ask, what letter 'a' says, pretending for the moment that it can say something. There is then the problem of which one of the many sounds of 'a' recognised by the phonics teacher is the right one in a particular instance. Suppose that we went further and agreed that in a particular word it was the 'short' sound as in 'scan' and 'sat'. Try reading this last sentence aloud. What sound corresponded to the 'a' in 'and'? Was it the same sound as we have just attributed to 'can' and 'sat'? Does not the sound vary with where 'and' comes in a larger environment? If 'and' had been the first word of an utterance, it would have been pronounced differently. Now consider 'occurrence'. What sound does the first 'e' make? Look at 'admittance'. What sound does the second 'a' make? What sound does the 'o' make in 'theory'? One could go on to give thousands of examples where the actual sound does not correspond to any of the alternatives offered by the teacher. It seems that the confusion that afflicts teachers may beget a similar confusion in children — with this difference: the child is likely to be at, and not past, a vital stage in his reading development. What seems simple, or ignorable, or allowable to the experienced reader may be utterly bewildering to the learner and it may put his future as a reader at risk.

In summary, I would suggest that the teacher should be aware both that phonics could only ever be a partial answer to reading problems, and further that it is full of difficulties all of which are more difficult to the learner than to the expert. I should like to suggest that at the most phonic work should be limited to:

(1)   the initial sounds of words met in their environment; and
(2)   drawing the attention of children to groups of words which have common patterns of spelling and of alleged sounds.

Word recognition and phonic approaches both obscure the major strategies that the child will have to learn to use if he is to become a successful reader. These strategies need to come into play as soon as the child begins to move out of the transition stage. In fact, it is using them that will take him out of that stage, for he will have used analogous strategies in processing speech. Thus we may be faced with a very odd situation indeed. The teacher who works only through whole word or phonic approaches, or through a mixture of both, runs the very serious risk of never paying attention to the fundamental skills of reading. It is very possible to have a situation in which the teacher works hard with phonic and whole-word strategies but in which the child has to teach himself to read, without much relevant guidance — or else fail.

The teacher is not helped here by adequate analyses of the reading process. An example of such inadequacy is the division of reading into stages such as initial, intermediate and advanced. It is true, of course, that children can become better at reading but it is at least open to doubt whether such stages have any reality outside the minds of their inventors and protagonists. The mistake lies in thinking that there are bundles of skills which belong to the initial stage of reading and which are appropriately to be learned then, and that there are similarly identifiable skills for each of the intermediate and advanced stages. In such models, it is easy to omit or to misplace skills. This is precisely what many of them do, and in the process they seem to underwrite the establishment of word recognition and perhaps also of phonic skills and to rate them as more valuable than they really are.

This present section began as a plea for giving a child a free choice of reading book and, therefore, for the ending of an era which the commercial primer dominated. When effective criteria are set up by which to judge them, such books often fall far short of what the child's interests demand. This is true both in the short run and in the longer term when the attitudes formed in his early encounters with books determine whether he is going to be an effective, fluent and skilful reader with a high regard for books, or whether he is going to reject them or relegate them to a place of only very minor importance in his life.

But, although a free choice of book will get a child around many difficulties, it is still the case that someone must make the book available to him in the first place and so his choice is necessarily from among books that others have previously selected. This brings us to the question of how such books should be chosen in the first place — and the answer is very simple — because of their merit as books, because of the quality of the writing and the illustrations, because they are worthwhile as literature or as sources of interesting information (or both) at the child's level. Although there has been improvement, some primers, even today, are too boring or too insipid to be treated seriously — poor texts accompany poor illustrations. When a primer is good as literature, then it, too, can be made available among the books from which a child makes his choice. But this does not mean that the notion of 'graded' readers should be accepted, even with the refinement of colour coding. As a rule, graded readers do not embody a tenable notion of what gradients in reading ability really are.

Element (4): help from the teacher

This section deals with what the teacher can do, and with what she can get the children to do, in order to develop reading. So as to put this in perspective, it returns to the question of what reading really is, and it takes up the notion of skills in general and reading skills in particular, so that the teacher's role can be defined in relation to this analysis. Before that, the large question of the 'reading environment' is considered. This includes both the physical setting and the general atmosphere in which learning to read actually takes place. Finally, some techniques for helping children are considered in two parts. The first, under the heading of the reading conference deals with some of the things that can be done with individual children on a day-to-day basis. The second deals with work with groups of children.

The reading environment

This section deals with what the staff as a whole can do to secure the best environment for reading. This is partly a matter of physical resources — of space and furniture and their use — and partly a matter of attitudes, particularly as they are exemplified in practice.

We begin with a simple question about where books should be kept. Do we want books to be in separate book corners, one for each class, or in a central library? The answer, in my view, is also simple. It is 'both'.

The reasons are partly practical. Some books need to be close at hand, perhaps because they are wanted for frequent use by a class; others, because of their rarity or price, might be kept centrally, especially if there is likely to be a demand for them from more than one class.

A classroom without a book corner lacks both a declaration of faith in books and a resource that can, amongst other things, be highly decorative. Libraries, in contrast, spell out their message rather more grandly. Each library is a token that great treasure-houses of the imagination and a near-infinity of knowledge exist and are accessible. Both book corners and libraries need to be visually exciting, and it is therefore fortunate that books lend themselves to colourful display.

The book corner should be carpeted and cushioned. The right place for children is, at least occasionally, on the floor —provided that it is comfortable. Children should be able to loll about without having to put up with the discomforts of furniture, especially of wooden furniture, which can be painful to those without much flesh on their bones. Libraries need to be organised with different purposes in mind and with the classification, storage and retrieval of information as major considerations.

The choice of materials and of books needs all the expertise that can be mustered. Public libraries are often willing to help and to supplement the school's resources by supplying books in bulk for

85

varying periods of time. Many are able also to supply batches of books, on demand, to deal with particular topics. Their children's librarians are usually real treasures, being anxious to meet the needs of teachers and generous with both their time and expertise.

With or without such outside help, a heavy burden will always fall on the school staff. I have already suggested that as many people as possible should be brought into the process of selecting books for reading aloud to children. The principle needs to be extended into the business of selecting books for class and library purposes. As part of the concerns of school management, time should be allocated for discussing choices, determining priorities, assigning resources and for reporting follow-up investigations into the use of the books. All staff will need access to catalogues and they will need to know where the books can be seen before they are purchased. Booksellers and publishers are usually willing to help. All these 'routes' and aids are important, but most important of all is that teachers should be encouraged to read widely to get first-hand knowledge of what is available for their children and to develop enthusiasms which they can transmit to them.

Books, of course, are the heart of the physical resources, but they are not all. Display materials, shelving and other furniture, catalogues and library signposts need to be selected with just as much care.

Attitudes are also important. These are shown through behaviour and, having been shown, are sometimes transmitted to others who might not themselves be fully aware of what is happening. The care and thoroughness which the staff give to the selection, keeping and display of books exemplify their attitudes. So, most importantly, does their willingness to be involved. The silent message that goes forth is something like this: 'Our book corners and libraries are very dear to us because they allow us to offer to children something that will bring them the very greatest pleasure and abiding interests, and which will be right at the heart of their growth into becoming educated and imaginative people.' Such attitudes cannot be 'taught' in any narrow, didactic way, but they can be transmitted and thus learned.

The reading conference

This section argues that all children should have regtular and fre-quent 'conferences' with their teacher. However, this sounds rather stern and I should like to keep the 'regular and frequent' and to change 'conferences' to 'chats'. To accept that there should be a conference or chat is to reject the notion that the main use of the teacher's time should be spent in listening to children read. Instead, it suggests what might happen at such conferences. In doing so it carries forward the examination of the reading process that was begun earlier and asks the question: what can the teacher do to help? It is the answers to this question that provide the teacher with the agenda for the reading conferences, that give her something to chat about.

There can be little doubt that listening to children read is an overrated pastime. To some extent it is a product of the teacher's word-fixation. When she hears children read, the teacher's basic habit is to listen for halts or errors and then to supply whatever word is causing difficulty or to get the child to 'sound it out'. In this way the teaching of reading comes to a very low-level activity which calls for very little expertise. Listening to children read can *occasionally* be useful, but there are many more interesting and profitable ways for the teacher to spend her time. This would be reason enough to abandon or, at least to curtail, the practice, but there is another reason; it reduces the scope given to the child and gives him false notions of what reading actually is. It is to this idea that we now turn.

The reading process and the process of learning to read

The principal goal of the school's work in the reading element of its language policy can be stated quite simply: it is to produce reading competence in its children. What, then, do we meant by 'reading competence'?

In the first place, reading is skilled behaviour. Skills, whether they are psychomotor skills such as walking, hammering, dancing and handwriting, or cognitive skills such as reading, have several things in common. All have to be learned. All have a repetitive element of some sort in the sense that skilled behaviour, once learned, may be repeated — and this with increasing ease and fluency. Further they are adaptive. Although they are repetitive, what is repeated is not necessarily completely identical with what has been done before. Thus a footballer, who is an expert kicker, may find that each ball that he kicks is a little different, or that it comes to him with a different spin, across ground that is not precisely the

87

same as any he has met before. The wind and weather change from time to time, as does the light. The pace at which he is compelled to run before he kicks will differ with the circumstances of the play. It is in the nature of skills that, within certain limits, the more practised the behaviour, the more likely it is that successful adaptations can be made.

Another feature of skills is that they tend not to be simple by their very nature. A step down a kerb may seem simple enough, but it entails using skills of walking that have been built up through months or years of practice. It involves complicated messages going from the eye to the brain and then to sets of effector muscles. These messages are about the length of the stride down the kerb, about the way the weight should be distributed, about preliminary strides and recovery strides and so on. All the while the operation is monitored by the individual so that minor and precise adaptations can be made as the operation progresses. This account is in fact much oversimplified — a great deal more actually goes on. But it allows us to make the point that, if walking off a pavement is so involved, how much more complicated is reading — which has within it as a minor element its own psychomotor component — likely to be. It also illustrates the fact that many examples of skilled behaviour are really sequences of other skilled behaviour co-ordinated, or as Bruner puts it 'orchestrated', into a whole. The skill of riding a two-wheel bicycle is another example of this. It would be misleading to call it simply a motor skill. One doubts whether such things as motor skills really exist. Like stepping down from the kerb, it is a psychomotor skill. It involves separable skills of balancing, of propelling, that is of applying force in a downwards and yet rotating movement, and steering — which includes the combination of redirecting the handlebars and leaning. Learning each of these subskills is not a matter of learning something unchanging like memorising a fact; it involves also learning to adapt and to adjust. Information about balance, which may be affected by the terrain, is acted upon very quickly. If there is overreaction, then there must be subsequent compensation. Pedalling is adjusted according to the road speed required, the gradient, if any, and the type of road surface. Steering also depends on messages about the direction wanted and about any obstacles in the way. All the time such skills are being used, feedback is being taken from several sources — eyes, ears, vestibular mechanism and so on.

A further point is that skilled behaviour is very easy — when you know how. Some amusing individuals take the normal processes of learning and combining further than is usual and indulge in ever more complicated skills — trick riding, juggling whilst riding — the sorts of things that one sees in circuses. Occasionally, individuals find coordination difficult, perhaps because of some pathological condition. One American president, himself a former athlete and male model, could not (it was alleged) walk and chew gum at the same time! Most of us would find it so easy that it would become automatic, but not unless there had been prior practice.

The matter of automaticity in behaviour is an interesting one. It comes about when we behave in certain complicated ways either without any, or with only a minimum of, conscious thought about the process. (The matter was discussed in Chapter 4 in connection with handwriting.) Thus the footballer does not have a discussion with himself about where to put his feet as he runs up to the ball, or about the force he should use when he kicks it. He begins, it seems, with some sort of intention, and the rest seems to happen. The same applies to the motorist. He uses many skills in orchestrated forms. To the extent that he is skilled, he does not need to pay more than minimal attention to the business of gear-changing or of steering. But he has the option and ability to override his automatic sequences; he can give conscious attention to, and alter, his braking, his steering or his manipulation of the gear-lever.

Such attention is very important. It becomes possible when we countermand the automatic. But there is also a less conscious sort of attention which is being paid as skills operate. This is monitoring. In a fairly detached way, we keep an eye, or an ear on the process that is going on automatically ready to modify its exercise if it should become necessary. Thus we set ourselves up to receive feedback which is essential alike to the exercise of a mature skill, to the learning of that skill and to its orchestration with other skills.

Taking feedback can also be a more conscious and organised affair. Many athletic performers (and artists such as singers and dancers) are aware that their skills may deteriorate, sometimes almost imperceptibly, over a period of time. This is why even top athletes who are by definition superbly skilled and coordinated have their coaches, why opera singers have their teachers, and why ballet dancers go to class every day. Yet they may all be far better performers than their teachers. Why, then, do they bother? The answer is 'feedback' and using it involves more than an ongoing self-monitoring and self-adjustment; this sort of feedback entails an interruption of the exercise of a skill in order to pay attention to it and possibly to modify it in practice.

Feedback, then, is most important for the learning and exercise of skills. Reading is skilled behaviour and so feedback is important to it as well. It can come from one or both of two directions. The first is from the performer himself, the second is from 'outside', from teachers and coaches. It can be used as part of normal 'automatic' functioning (as when the cyclist takes in the feedback information that he is overbalancing and takes corrective action to adjust), or it can be used to break in upon the 'automatic', and to pay selective attention to some part of the skilled sequence perhaps with the aim of altering it or improving its performance.

Reading is best seen as an organised skill which includes sub-skills. The psychomotor element to which referred, and which involves skilled eye-movement, is one of these. It is also cognitive in the sense that information is sought and taken in and processed constructively along with other information that is already in the long-term memory.

There is a respect in which reading differs in degree from the other orchestrated skills that we mentioned before such as driving a car, riding a bicycle and so on. It is not that they are simple, while reading is complex. Reading — and listening too — has the characteristic that it is much more open-ended than driving a car or riding a bicycle. Consequently, it is much harder to identify a target behaviour and to say that it is the invariable goal that must be attained. In reality few skills are not open-ended to some degree. That is why we stressed earlier that they must be adaptive. All of them utilise knowledge. All operate in varying circumstances. The knowledge that reading incorporates is extremely varied and, in a very significant sense, is limitless. And the circumstances in which it operates — different sorts of confrontations with different sorts of text — are qualitatively different from the circumstances, changing as they are, in which people drive cars and ride bicycles. As has been shown, the footballer, kicking a ball, is always in a unique situation. But that sort of uniqueness is trivial when one compares it to the difference between reading Russian and reading English, or with reading a text dealing with advanced economics and reading one on car engineering.

At this stage it is necessary to make a distinction that will illuminate our concerns. It begins with an anecdote.

Some years ago one of my responsibilities was to organise short courses for teachers in the use of audiovisual aids. They were taught to thread film and tape, to operate projectors and tape machines, to play both video and audio machines, to use blackboards and whiteboards and so on. Judged from one point of view, none of these is a simple skill. It is true that they become easier with practice, but each involves several subskills arranged more or less sequentially. The technicians involved in the course were good communicators and they soon had the least confident of the teachers operating skilfully. Thus many teachers became competent. I call their competence 'competence A'.

But there was another sort of competence, one which was even more complex. This involved using audiovisual aids but not just in the sense of being able to connect up, thread, focus, and to switch on and switch off at the right moment. What is involved in this other competence is knowing, in addition, whether, when, and in what manner to use the aids. This competence I call 'competence B'. My technicians could offer only limited help with this because the exercise of competence B required that a much wider range of considerations than they were used to dealing with had now to be taken into account. It became necessary to be able to decide, for example, whether, if information was to be transmitted to a group, it was best (or even possible) to do it using audiovisual aids, or whether it was better to use some other technique such as telling them the information by word of mouth. Thus competence B always includes competence A but works at a higher level of sophistication. The distinction is important in at least two related aspects. Teaching and learning competence B involves the teacher in doing more than would the teaching and learning of competence A. The reading programme should take this into account and the language policy should make a clear distinction between the two.

Remembering what was said about simple and advanced skills, we can say that competence B is more advanced than competence A, but that both are made up of equally complex skills. Reading, we have said, is the construing of meaning from print, and there is no way in which this can ever be regarded as a simple skill. This, incidentally, makes us doubt the accuracy and usefulness of so-called hierarchical models of reading skills — those which purport to identify separate initial, intermediate and advanced skills, for example.

A further refinement needs to be added to the picture. Just as there is an open-endedness about reading in the sense that it can result in the construing of very different sorts of meaning depending upon the text that is being read, so there can be a similar sort of diversity in the purposes for which reading is undertaken in the first place. For example, there is the sort of reading which is intended to construe as full a version of meaning as is reasonably possible, given the text. Then there are other sorts of behaviour which are not intended to result in this full meaning but rather to check whether a text contains a particular item, or to ascertain its general drift. These processes are usually described as skimming, scanning, and so on. It seems quite clear that they, too, can properly be called reading but that they are partial rather than complete. They are incomplete in the sense that they truncate the construing process, and also because their samplings of text for attention are selected on a different principle. This selection is part of competence B rather than competence A.

Where does this take us? Again, we must insist that reading is about the construing (or, if one prefers the term, the construction) of meaning. In other words, there is no reading that does not involve comprehension. 'Reading' of the sort that takes place during the transitional stage, or when someone who does not understand a text nevertheless 'reads' it aloud, or when someone who does not understand, say, French, but knows enough to 'read' it aloud, is not reading at all but is cross-moding. Other examples of cross-moding occur when we take down, perhaps impeccably, dictation about a topic of which we are completely ignorant. Useful cross-moding takes place when the teacher writes down something that a child has composed orally and when a child merely gives the spoken version for writing that he does not yet understand. The important principle here is that one should never mistake cross-moding for real reading, though, as we said earlier, one can merge into the other.

Real reading involves construing meaning from written or printed texts and that is what children have to learn to do. Further, they need to construe meaning from different sorts of written texts, from poems as well as newspapers, from personal letters as well as from business letters, from notices, from labels as well as from books. They need to understand that writing tends to work differently in different genres; that each genre has its cluster of styles, some of which it may share with other genres but which, taken all together, are what makes it a genre. They need to understand that reading may be for different purposes, and when one has decided what that purpose is, one adjusts one's reading behaviour accordingly.

Helping the individual

In school the scarcest commodity is the teacher's time. So it is very important that it is well-used. As far as the reading programme is concerned, this means looking at what the child needs to make progress towards becoming a competent reader and then deciding exactly what the teacher can do to help.

In a sense skills, including reading, cannot really be 'taught', but there is no doubt that people can be helped to acquire them. One of the worst ways of helping children is to 'hear children read'. This may seem to be a very surprising statement to make about what is, after all, a staple part of the reading programme in many classes. However, what 'hearing children read' means to one teacher is not the same as it means to another. To some, it means supplying words that children do not know or which they get wrong as they read to the teacher from their books (which are usually primers). Often, the teachers base their interventions on assumptions about the nature of reading which stem from what we earlier called 'a word-fixated' view. Closely related to them are other teachers who may not immediately supply a word when the child is in difficulty. Instead, they suggest that it should be 'sounded out'. They, too, base their intervention on a word-fixated view. Right at the other side of the spectrum are those who use the opportunity to talk to the child about his difficulties, about the book, and not just about his mistakes as he tries to read it. In other words, they use the occasion as a conference, or to chat, and not as an inquisition. When this happens the teacher immediately begins to operate at a higher professional level. It shows that it is possible to devote the time that other teachers use for listening to quite other purposes. My suggestion is that merely listening and supplying words and getting children to 'sound out' should become less usual activities and only a small part of the repertoire that the teacher uses to help children. If the idea of a regular conference is adopted, listening to a child might occasionally be part of that encounter. There are many other valuable possibilities, some of which are listed below. Of course, what actually happens at the conference ought to depend on the teacher's estimation of the child's needs. If the child can be encouraged to talk about any of his needs so much the better, and these, too, might be met.

(1)   continuing the collaborative activity of the transitional stage. At that stage, it will be remembered, the teacher was the co-producer of a text, the scribe for a composer who could not yet handwrite or spell. Transitional reading can proceed side by side with true reading until well past the time when the true reading is firmly established. During the early stages of

reading the child needs much support and reading a text can be a joint, collaborative venture;

(2) extending the child's understanding of what reading is through discussion and by example. In order to emerge beyond the transition stage, a child needs to understand what reading is and how to go about doing it. Part of the purpose of the interview is to make sure that the child's model of reading becomes more sophisticated, that it extends beyond understanding the differences between 'tell' and 'read' into understanding such matters as the nature of digits and how to 'read' them, and on into strategies for construing meanings from texts;

(3) extending the child's knowledge of the written mode of language and especially of the different genres and styles that are contained within it. These include such matters as the formal layout of different kinds of writing such as poems, notices, letters, particular ways of starting and finishing, of introducing characters, setting scenes and sequencing what is written. There are obvious links here with the child's progress in writing;

(4) discussing the child's choice of reading matter and extending his range by giving trailers and by using some of the time to read to him;

(5) discussing the child's reading experience in general. The child could keep a diary in which he listed with brief comments all the important matter that he read. This could form the basis for broad reviews of his experience as a reader;

(6) discussing what he has read in detail. An excellent way of finding out whether a child has understood what he has 'read' is to elicit an account of it during the course of discussion. Ideally, of course, such a request will not be made on any inquisitorial spirit. Instead, it will be a matter of one reader sharing pleasure and information with another;

(7) dealing with specific techniques for construing meaning. Of all these, that of forming broad expectations about what meanings the text seems about to signal comes first. Such expectations come from using various kinds of knowledge. For example, knowledge of the genre and its cluster of appropriate styles is helpful. Knowing what has gone before is also valuable in making intelligent guesses. Understanding that what is meant and the way it is put in the first part of a sentence governs what can come is a major insight. In other words,

the child must be taught to use whole-text clues and in-text clues, grammatical or syntactical clues and so-called semantic or meaning clues. As one progresses in any utterance, what one can go on to say or write is limited by the sorts of grammatical construction one has already embarked upon and also by the other signals of meaning that one has already made. Above all, though, the child needs to come to come to understand that while making informed and intelligent guesses and then confirming or informing them by further attention to the text is a vital thing for him to do, there is nothing infallible about it. He can go wrong. Sometimes, indeed, he *will* go wrong. The fact that he does go wrong is really a credit to him, for it shows that he is working in the right way. When he thinks that he has gone wrong, however, the main consideration is for him to check and then, if necessary, to correct himself. In this way, dealing with expectations reinforces what he will have learned in (2) above when suggestions for deepening his understanding of the reading process were made;

(8) using more specific techniques. The teacher will understand that, especially for the inexperienced reader, slow reading is practically an impossiblility. Very slow reading, especially item by item reading, puts almost unbearable burdens on the short-term memory. Short-term memory is a dynamic process of temporarily retaining items, limited both in overall capacity and in its ability to hold items for long. In this respect, reading is again a little like riding a bicycle. It is very difficult and, indeed, almost impossible to ride it below a certain speed. This, as was pointed out earlier, is another reason why teachers should not rely on methods which unnecessarily slow children down — such as the sounding out and subsequent blending of the sounds of a word. The techniques that a child can use if he runs into difficulties include such suggestions as to:

(a) re-read,
(b) read faster,
(c) go further on in the text to see if meaning emerges or if any more clues are given,
(d) go further back in the text to pick up the earlier meanings.

If these successive ploys fail then the child can:

(e) try the initial sounds corresponding to the first letter of any word which is puzzling him,

(f) move further into the sound system and speak a whole chunk of text aloud (or 'say' it to oneself).

If these fail he must then either

(g) ask someone, or

(h) move on without solving the problem.

Much of this is showing the child how to treat larger bits of language than just words or even sentences. If the teacher remembers that the child's task is to get meaning out of language in texts, this will serve to orientate her thinking profitably. We shall return briefly to this theme when we deal with language and learning in Chapter 7. Here we urge that she should encourage the child to look for key sentences and key paragraphs such as those which announce what is to come or summarise what has gone.

Helping groups of children

In 1978, Her Majesty's Inspectors published the Primary Survey.* Among their most important judgements about reading was this:

> For the abler readers, at all ages, there was little evidence that more advanced reading skills were being taught. The work which the ablest readers were given to do was too easy in two-fifths of the classes. Children were asked to comment on what they had read in about one-third of the seven-year-old classes rising to three-fifths of the 11 year-old classes, but in only a very small minority of classes at any age were children discussing the books they had read at other than a superficial level of comprehension.

Now, it is quite clear that some of the activities recommended above would allow the teacher to offer help in precisely these areas.. Using clues of all kinds to arrive at meaning and discussing books and parts of books at some length meet the Inspectors' criticism head-on.

There is also a range of techniques that can be used with groups which would serve the same purpose. Group work on reading needs to be managed very carefully indeed if it is to be successful. In particular, there are two essential matters to which the teacher must give her attention, if there is to be hope of success. These are, first, the right choice of materials and, second, training the group in discussion techniques. Discussing in groups does not necessarily come easily to children. Most adults will recognise the feeling of apprehension that they themselves sometimes experience when they wish to make a contribution to a group discussion, perhaps at a staff or professional meeting. Children need to be helped to get over any such feelings as they may have. At the same time, as we shall see, it is very important that the discussions are not free-for-alls where any sort of thing can be said in any order. As we deal with the various group activities, we shall refer again both to the right choice of materials and to the management of discussion.

Broadly, there are three sorts of group activity that will serve the purpose of helping children to learn how to get meaning out of texts. When they work well, they have several other features that are helpful to the child's language development and also to his intellectual and cognitive skills. They are: group deletion (cloze) work; group sequencing work; and group prediction work.

Group deletion (cloze) work

Cloze procedures can, of course, be managed at both individual and group levels. They are commonly thought to have two purposes: the first has to do with the notions of the reading ability of an individual; the second with the readability of a text; the one with weighing up what an individual can do and the other with what a text contains that makes it easy or difficult to read. My own view about reading ability is that it is not in general well-understood, and so I look with some suspicion on the use of cloze as an indicator of reading ability. It is true that doing cloze does actually call for reading ability, but it is doubtful whether it should ever be used to measure that ability in quantitative terms (that is, by giving numerical scores which are supposed to be an index of ability). One's doubts about readability, which is the alleged *intrinsic* difficulty of a text and which a number of formulae have been devised to measure, are even more pronounced. There may be some value in it, but I believe that it is essentially the result of a misconception about the nature of texts and their place in the reading process. However, these are controversial matters and there is no space to pursue them here and now. From what I have said, though, it will be clear that I do not advocate the use of cloze procedures as measures of either reading ability or 'readability'. But there is another use for cloze that is highly pertinent to our purpose: it is to train people in reading skills. The skills that it emphasises are those of picking up and using clues to the construction of meaning, which, we have insisted, is central to the whole business of reading.

Essentially, cloze involves the systematic deletion of parts of a text which, deletions and all, children are then asked to read. The deletions may in principle be of two kinds. The more unusual kind is when certain sorts of words are deleted. For example, one might take a poem and delete some, or all, of the adjectives. The ensuing discussion would involve children putting forward their suggestions for each of the missing adjectives in turn. The object is to teach about literary style and the choice of words — either style in general or that of a particular poet. Similar strategic deletions can be made in 'information' texts with the object of improving the understanding of the reader as he deliberates the puzzles of the missing words and ponders about the meaning of the text.

The other, more usual, type of cloze exercise involves the deletion of every fifth, sixth, seventh, tenth, twentieth, or whatever, word. In general, a passage becomes harder to understand the higher the proportion of words deleted.

As we said above, the choice of text is important. It should be one in which there is a fair chance of the children becoming interested. It may or may not be literary. The proportion of words to be deleted depends on the teacher's understanding of her children. It is best to begin with a low rate, say one-in-ten. When the deletion has been done, the teacher needs to look at the result. Ideally, it should be obvious what most of the missing words are. There should also be room for discussion of alternatives.

The essential thing to remember is that the real object of the exercise is not at all to be able to find the 'correct' word that is missing from the slot; it is to incite discussion based on close scrutiny of a text and to identify and to discuss the clues which lie behind all the suggestions for filling the gap.

The procedure might be along these lines: the teacher, having chosen a passage, made deletions and numbered each deletion for ease of reference, gives a copy to each child. The children are told that this is a game and it is one which will help them to become better readers because it gives them practice in doing certain things. They are also told that they will not be allowed to write anything down during the game. What they have to do is to suggest a suitable word for each space in turn. They are then asked to read the passage and told not to worry if they cannot guess any of the missing words.

About six to eight children seem to constitute an appropriate group. The teacher will need to be present and to take an active part.

She begins the discussion by asking for a suggestion for filling the first gap. The children must understand that they are not allowed to call out. When they have reached a conclusion privately, they can indicate by showing their hand. The teacher then picks a child. Some gaps will be easier to fill than others and so she can match the task to the child and select a child who is likely to make a reasonable answer. In this way the method lends itself to use with groups whose members may show a range of attainment. Once an 'answer' has been offered, the teacher needs to ask 'Why have you made that suggestion? What is it that made you think so?' As a rule, the answer will be on the lines of 'It seemed to make sense,' or even 'That's the sort of word that's needed here,' meaning that the child has made a suggestion for repairing a grammatical structure, perhaps by supplying the right part of speech (noun, verb, etc). It is then essential for that suggestion to be discussed before going on further. The children should come to realise that in some cases there is no right or wrong answer and that what they are dealing with is degrees of appropriateness. At the same time, they are exercised in identifying and using clues of several kinds. These clues might be from the genre, or from the author's style, or from the way a sequence seems to be progressing, judged by the semantic and grammatical constraints it has already imposed. The point is that they are making intelligent guesses on the basis of what they know. They are forming expectations about meaning and the discussion shows what clues they have picked up. It also shows others in the group what clues it is possible, in principle, to pick up. In other words, it teaches them how to read.

The teacher should try to get a group to reach a consensus. She should then reveal what the missing word actually was, emphasising that this was not necessarily inevitable but that it was the author's choice. The discussion can then begin again. Was this the best or the only word that would do? Again, opinions are one thing and reasons are another and it is reasons, and thus argument, that the teacher is seeking.

As time goes on, there can be an increase in difficulty either by choosing a text that is more remote from the children's experience or by making a greater proportion of deletions. Of course, the purpose is not to frustrate but to exercise and the teacher will find that there is value in discussing even 'easy' suggestions.

Cloze procedures are, then, a valuable technique. But they are at best an extra to the business of real reading. Perhaps the best way to use them is in short bursts — perhaps two or three clozes, three or four times a year.

Group sequencing work

Group sequencing is perhaps most suitable for groups of older juniors. It, too, will need the involvement of the teacher, at least during the first few discussions, but if there has been work on cloze discussions beforehand, the teacher may find that the children soon fall into the routine and can manage without her presence. Nevertheless, her contribution will in any case be vital, for she has to select and prepare appropriate material and also to train groups in the ways to proceed.

The material may be an article or a story, or a part of either. The original is then divided into sections, perhaps with a few sentences or a paragraph in each section. Each section needs to be written separately on its own sheet of paper. The reason for this is that we are not asking the children to do a sort of jigsaw puzzle. Any clues as to the correct sequence should come from the text itself and from the general knowledge that each child brings to the text and not from the shape of the paper or from the marks of scissor cuts.

A complete set is given to each child with each section numbered randomly. The children are told that the object of the exercise is to put the sections into the best order. At first they work in pairs and each pair is asked to produce a sequence that they have agreed through discussion. Pairs can then be combined into fours and, whenever possible, pairs that have produced different results can now be put together. If any of the new groups still disagree with the conclusion reached by another group, the process of combining can be repeated.

Finally, the original order is revealed and discussed. Again, it is this discussion element that is the real aim of the exercise. 'What made you think that that would come next?' is the classic question. Some of the answers will be in the text, others will be in the children's prior knowledge. Sometimes they will have to make inferences, and making inferences is another essential skill in the business of understanding. In such cases, that is, they will know because they have inferred.

Some inferences are easy and obvious:

In a little house there lived two rabbits.

How does one know that there was a little house? No statement is made to that effect. Nevertheless there is a very obvious implica-tion to that effect.

At other times one makes inferences of an intermediate sort:

The leaves were falling as John set out.

The question here is: what time of the year was it? The inference is now a conditional one and the answer 'probably autumn'. 'Prob-ably', because it was not certain; leaves could have been falling, for some reason, at a different time of the year.

Such inferences are part of the normal reading process. Sequen-cing in the way suggested will allow children to make them, to discuss them, and thus to demonstrate to their peers one of the strategies for getting meaning that they, too, can use.

Group sequencing can be fun. But it should not be attempted too often — perhaps as often as cloze procedures, but only if it turns out to be enjoyable.

Group prediction work

Group prediction work is similar in some respects to group sequen-cing. Once again, the choice of material is vital. Once again, the aim is reasoned discussion, rather than merely coming up with the answers. Once again, the purpose is to develop the children's own insights into the ways in which authors work, into the clues that reside in the text, and into the ways in which it is possible to make intelligent guesses to make meanings.

Briefly, the best procedure is to select a group of children who may be mixed in ability and large in number. One has seen the technique work, apparently effectively, with classes of 30 and more.

The teacher divides a passage into instalments. Again there should be no 'irrelevant' clues such as those that might be provided by a jigsaw effect. The first instalment is then given out and the children are asked to say what they think might come next. They can make any suggestion, provided that they can support it by making some reference to the text in their possession. Of course, this is very open-ended and there is room, as a rule, for many sensible proposals. The next instalment is then given out and the children are asked if they wish to change their expectations of what is still to come and, if so, what the clues are that cause them to wish to do so. The same procedure is then followed with the next instalment, and so on.

The teacher's choice, as we said, is vital. The instalments should be roughly of equal length and each should ideally help to clarify but not finally resolve the meaning of the whole, so that there is a cumulative process of making hypotheses that are consistent with what is already supplied, testing these hypotheses in the light of new material, modifying them if necessary and then repeating the whole process.

Monitoring

On the whole, attempts to monitor individual children and to survey the attainment of whole cohorts of children have been spoiled by an understanding of both reading and of learning to read that has been grossly inadequate. If one is not sure, or if one is simply wrong, about either of these, then it can never be possible to monitor reading progress properly. After all, how can we assess something if we do not know what it is that we are assessing? The plain fact is that any view of reading which does not give the central place to meaning and any view of the process of learning to read which does not give the central place to learning to arrive at meaning from print are both lethal and make attempts to assess or monitor potentially misleading.

On the other hand, once meaning is given this central role, we can then look at the means that are available to cope with it. Word recognition has its own small part to play, but, as I have pointed out, there are real dangers in word-fixated approaches and in the commercial materials that are founded upon them. Phonics, too, may have a place. But it can only be a small one and we need to remember that it is founded on misconceptions and distortions. It may, as a result, cause more frustrations than it relieves. Not everyone agrees with this view but, whether they do or not, it is absolutely important that we all recognise that there are other skills to reading and that we identify these and give children help in learning them.

Reference

Primary Education in England (1975) (HMSO, London)

6

The Development of Writing

The goal of that part of the language policy which deals with writing can be stated very simply. It is for the child to achieve first autonomy and then increasing competence as a writer. Autonomy means the ability to compose language that is truly *written* and not just spoken language written down. Competence is the ability to use language to express, to record and to communicate meanings. It will involve the writer in increasing his ability to communicate with others in different genres, and for different purposes while using a repertoire of styles that are suitable for different tasks.

Autonomy also has another aspect. If it is to be achieved, it will mean writing independently of the teacher, so that her function as a scribe and as the main supplier of spellings is left far behind.

Continuities and discontinuities

Written language has its own distinctive characteristics. Some of them were dealt with in Chapters 2 and 4. With these in mind, it is possible to say that, while spoken language is the basis for the development of written language, there are considerable differences between the two modes. And so it is the case that when the child learns to write he has to learn to cope with both continuities and discontinuities.

The continuities are part of a chain of learning which links early personal interactions to prelinguistic attributions of intention and meaning, then to the communication of meanings and then to the clothing of such intentions in words and sound patterns, some of which are invented by the child but which soon come to utilise the mother tongue. To the extent that writing is built on speaking and

103

listening, it follows that all the antecedent and contingent conditions for the development of spoken language should ideally have been met if writing is to develop in its turn. This instances once again the interrelatedness of the language skills which was one of the most important reasons for devising a language policy.

However, there are other foundations which also seem to be necessary for the development of writing. The differences which distinguish writing as a mode from spoken language have to be learned and such learning has its own developmental antecedents. Putting it another way, we can say that if the child has been successful in learning to speak and to listen, he is to that extent well-placed to learn to write, but that there is more to learn and the preparation for this new learning needs to be established in good time, for it, too, involves earlier learning.

Lev Vygotsky has made a most striking contribution to our understanding of such learning. He emphasised the importance of speech both in its own right and as a powerful system which tends to influence other learning. He asserted that the other roots of writing lie in activities such as drawing and gesture. Drawing becomes the 'drawing' of language. Gesture becomes specialised into writing. Other sources of writing are said to be storytelling and pretend-play. We shall return to these two later. For the moment it is enough to indicate that for anyone not convinced by Vygotsky the activities that he saw as being significant have developmental value in other respects, too, so that parents and teachers who encourage them can do so on the grounds that they are likely to prove to be highly productive.

Though there are real differences between the modes, it would be unwise to overstress them. When the child comes to read and write, he will use the words and grammar that he has acquired through speaking and listening. Unless he has had access to the distinctive words, grammar and styles of written language through listening (as stories are read to him), he will have no option but to use what is his only resource — the words and grammar of spoken language. This is a major reason why the parents should read to the child.

It is the case that neither mode is monolithic — there are variations of genre within each. Some sorts of spoken language are nearer to written language than are others. It was with this in mind that we suggested that long utterances should be included among the areas of competence that we should want each child to master in speech. 'Long utterances' are either monologues or protracted contributions to conversation which have many of the attributes of monologue. Long utterances in this sense are valuable precisely because they are likely to be in sentence form and also because they raise for the utterer problems of coherence or thematic unity, and of cohesion or textual unity. The solutions to these problems — sequencing and avoiding undue irrelevance, for example, and maintaining a flow from sentence to sentence so that genuine text results — are solutions that will become applicable in the child's writing. In this sense, it is not merely previously learned words and grammar but also principles of organisation and unity that will be learned first in speech and then incorporated into writing.

Perhaps the toughest lesson that the child has to learn about writing is that it is hard work. Autonomy means doing without the teacher as supplier of handwriting and spelling. Therefore it means undertaking burdens for himself. Even when handwriting becomes automatic, it remains a tiring activity. Spelling, once it too becomes automatic, is not so much of a problem, but until that stage is reached it presents constant difficulty. The child deals with this problem in one of several ways. He makes up his own spellings, devising his own systems for relating sounds to particular letters and letter order. Or he uses conventional spellings which he has come to know. Or he takes some pains to find out the conventional spelling from whatever sources he has been taught to use. In any case, it is a burden to him. In addition, he has to find some way of ordering what he wants to write. The longer the piece, the harder this is likely to be. This is where one of the principal discontinuities shows itself, for the spoken language to which he is most used is conversation. Conversation is marked by reciprocity, by being organised on the principle that what one speaker says helps to cue and to prompt the succeeding speaker. Connected writing of any length is, of course, quite different from this. Learning precisely how to go about making connections and, before that, coming to understand that such connections ought to be made, is something we shall go into later. For the moment, the point to be stressed is that hard work is inevitable when writing.

What the child sees in relation to handwriting is a teacher who can apparently write without any difficulty at all. Writing seems just to flow from her fibretip just as easily as talk comes from her lips. He is not to know that all adults find the business of writing physically and mentally tiring. Few grown-ups can write for long without feeling fatigue, and sometimes even pain and discomfort in the hand and arm. The long struggle of a writer to make good sense and to end with a truly connected text which at the same time may convey delicate meanings and have aesthetic value is something that is concealed from him. It is important, though, that he should come to regard it as the norm and, the more advanced he gets, to expect to review and revise his writing even to the extent of expecting to do several drafts when it really matters. This view of the complexity of getting to the finished product should gradually be impressed upon him. Later, we shall suggest some of the ways in which this might be done. At the transition stage such matters have no relevance. Once he is out of that stage they become more and more indispensable to the competent writer.

The need to review and revise is linked to the child's notion of genre and of purpose. The beginnings of the child's notion of appropriateness, which causes him to match his language to his sense of purpose and to his perception of genre is, once again, to be found in his previous knowledge of spoken language. It will be fed when he listens to stories and to other sorts of writing being read to him and also when he begins to read more extensively for himself. Thus, once again the different parts of the language policy can be seen as mutually supportive.

The second great lesson that the child must learn is that to be a competent writer, one must have command over sentences. It is not the case that the sentence is a *necessary* unit in spoken language. The normal unit of organisation there is the tone group. In writing, the balance is exactly opposite. It is quite possible to have writing that is not in sentence form. Lists, addresses, notices and headlines are cases in point. But for a whole range of writing the sentence is obligatory. It follows that getting children to write sentences is one of the major problems that the teacher has.

We shall now take some of these problems separately, but we should remember that language is a system and although we can take different aspects and discuss them separately, each aspect actually will influence the others. Thus we shall deal with the writing of sentences, and, in particular with the choice of words and grammatical systems and structures, with the organisation of writing, that is with getting ideas and ordering both them and the language which is selected as a result and, finally, with the shaping and styling of the writing to serve the purposes of the writer and to match its intended audience. But all are linked in practice and what the writer does in connection with one will always constrain what he can do in connection with the others.

Our way into these matters is first of all to outline the course of development that the ability to compose normally takes. Then we shall turn to what the teacher can do to foster this development.

The development of the ability to compose written language

Chapter 4 of this book dealt with what was there called the transitional stage of literacy which had several characteristics. The most notable of them was that while the child had the appearance of working in the written mode, that is of reading and writing, he was in reality working more in the spoken mode. What resulted was speech written down.

The line of development as far as writing is concerned is very clear; it is to achieve independence of speech and to compose language that is genuinely written language. Here, we can pause to sympathise with the teacher who has advised the child who is sucking his pencil and who is at a loss 'to write down what you would say'. Such advice is valid during the transitional stage, but it is exactly what we do not want when once he is out of that stage. The teacher who gives such advice may not understand the intrinsic differences between speech and writing, or that it is circumstances that determine whether it is appropriate to use the resources of one or of the other, or that there are psychologically different considerations which govern the composition and use of each mode.

As the child progresses towards autonomous writing, his relationship with the teacher will change. He will learn to handwrite and thus not be dependent on her to provide the very marks and substance of his writing. Gradually he will progress, too, from total dependence for his spellings towards self-reliance. This move forward may be accompanied by regression in other respects.

As he moves into independent writing, there is almost certain to be a reduction in the complexity of his composition compared with his spoken composition. The complexity of his speech is always likely to be underestimated. It is dynamically very involved. The interactions are subtle. The grammar is remarkable both in range and in power. His ability to cooperate in the making of meaning through conversation tends to be taken for granted because it is an everyday occurrence, even though remarkable results are achieved. Of course, not all talk is like this, but such features are common in the language of most children before they get to school. Perhaps because he is moving into new areas and trying new skills, the child drops the level of complexity. He cannot, in autonomous writing, rely on cues from his partner for he is now on his own. He has to cope with the problems of handwriting and serial letter order. It is true that he had to cope with somewhat analogous problems of articulating sounds in speech, but he had so much practice that it became like second nature to him. As a writer he must now take great care and expend great effort and make up his mind what to write without cues, all at the same time. Accordingly, it is no surprise that the level of structural complexity drops to a level at which he finds he can cope.

During the transitional stage there is a similar drop in complexity. At this time the teacher will probably take care that what the child composes is, or becomes, a sentence. Many teachers, indeed, find it difficult to lend their pencils to anything which is not a sentence. When the child is composing on his own, what he makes up may or may not be a sentence. He will be guided by what he has previously been used to making up and that may or may not be in sentence form. In its spoken version, it will have been uttered with an intonation pattern that both marked structure (as a potentially meaningful unit, not necessarily as a sentence), and itself helped the listener to construe meaning. Perhaps the most difficult task for the young composer is to move intonation away from this prominent place and into the background. When he does this he has to come to rely on making structures that will stand satisfactorily when isolated upon the page. Further, they must be of a conventionally approved type. When these criteria have been met such structures can be marked orthographically by an initial upper-case letter and a concluding full-stop. When we look at what the child actually does, we find movement in the right direction, but it may not always be a precisely coordinated movement. For example, he may be so anxious to oblige with his capital and full-stop that he uses them well before he is secure in using the sentence. Accordingly, there will be instances when these orthographic markers are 'incorrectly' used. Nevertheless, it would be most unwise to regard such incorrect uses as mistakes or errors. What they are is evidence that the child is trying to get his mind round some difficult notions (and, incidentally, to please adults in the process). Essentially, the problem of punctuating is one of understanding the grammatical structure which punctuation serves to mark. This is why the use of punctuation marks is so easy and yet so hard to teach. Anyone who has a sound understanding of structures will have little difficulty in learning to use them. Anyone who has no such grasp will find it impossible to use them properly. What we have with the child who is moving from the transitional stage into autonomous writing is something between total ignorance and absolute security. We should therefore expect some incorrect uses. Nevertheless, the teacher's strategy is the right one. It is to demonstrate the use of the capital and the full-stop at the transitional stage and then to get the child to use both as he copies what the teacher has written. Most teachers then go on steadily pointing out instances of sentences in the child's reading matter and indicating that they, too, are punctuated in this way. The child is then encouraged to use the same markers in his own writing. Whenever he writes a sentence that is not properly punctuated the teacher can, if she thinks the child is ready, point this out and either supply the punctuation herself or get the child to do so.

There is, it will be understood by all who have tried, no fast and easy way of getting a child either to write sentences or to mark them orthographically. The business is marked by partial understandings and by regressions when the child has other things on his mind. Yet the process is clear enough. Grammatically and structurally the establishment of the sentence is the most important step that the child will take in his development as a writer. Much is also clear about the help that he can be offered.

In the first place, it is certain that there is no way in which a definitional approach will work. Definitions of what sentences are, are often the subject of argument among professional linguists. This is not mainly because they are more argumentative than the rest of us. It is, rather, that the sentence itself is a varied and complicated thing to have a simple unequivocal definition. Most teachers, in the experience of the writer, are themselves unable to come up with a reasonably watertight definition, and when they do, they would not be understood by young children, because they usually rely on a prior understanding of such terms as 'subject', 'predicate', 'finite verb', and so on. Nor will such definitions as 'a sentence is a complete thought' help for they are no more than rubbish whose effect can only be to transfer the utterer's own confusion to the child. The truth of this particular matter is that there is no sense in which a sentence is necessarily 'a complete thought' and in any case such a definition would not mark off sentences from other structures which have just as much claim to embody 'complete thoughts'.

A second point about which we can be clear is that, although the sentence is the key grammatical structure in writing, writing sentences is not the only thing of merit that a child may accomplish when he writes. He may, for example, generate ideas for content and put them into sequence. He may exploit his vocabulary to send precise signals. Accordingly, when a teacher finds that a child is not using sentence structures securely, this does not exhaust all that the teacher can find that is remarkable or worthy of positive comment in the child's writing. Putting it another way, progression in writing is many-faceted. Ability to write sentences is in the long run vital, but the need to achieve this ability must not be allowed to stand in the way of the child's learning other important matters as well.

Gradually, the child's ability to write sentences will become more secure. But other skills will begin to make demands on him as well. His problem as a writer is not merely to write sentences. It is to learn to develop meanings over several sentences. In other words, he moves from the composition of single sentences to the composition of fuller texts. This raises the problems of how to achieve coherence and cohesion. Coherence is the unity of the text as far as subject-matter is concerned. Thus a story, if it is to be coherent, would have incidents arranged in what would basically be a chronological order, with such possible complications as, for instance, flashbacks or reminiscences which might disturb that sequence, but which are really also dependent on it. Descriptive details concerning the actors, the settings, and the events might be woven into this sequence at appropriate points. A set of instructions would be coherent if they took the subject matter and arranged it so that nothing of importance was omitted. Cohesion, on the other hand, is unity of language. It means that a text is not just a collection of sentences but a structure within which sentences are linked to each other. Coherence of subject matter and cohesion of language are not really separable in practice. The writer, in effect, accepts certain constraints such as those of writing sentences, and of achieving coherence of subject matter and cohesion of language simultaneously. He must, in other words, develop his subject matter in sentences that are linked to each other. This is a tall order. Doing it successfully is something that professional writers of considerable stature confess to finding difficult. Fortunately, the child has a device at hand that will help him to do the trick.

Children seem to find narrative intriguing. In its story and play forms, it plays a great part in their lives. The stories which, hopefully, they hear every day *are* narratives. Most of the play in which they engage and especially the pretend play is in narrative form, organised, that is, on the chronological principle — which gives coherence to children's writing. Children take to it readily and use it as an all-purpose organising principle. Thus they use it not merely to tell stories and make reports; they also employ it where adults might not, for instance, in 'pure' descriptions. If a child were asked to describe his classroom, there is a strong chance that he would use the chronological principle; 'First, I could see . . . . Then I could see . . .' and so on.

Here we move on a little too quickly, for the multi-purpose use of the principle is matched by the ubiquitous use of 'and' as a linking device to achieve continuity and therefore unity in the language. It is very possible for the teacher to look upon the use of 'and' with some disdain. Adults like to see variety both in sentence structure and in the ways in which sentences are linked to one another. From their point of view, the use of 'and' is a mark either of lack of resource or even of idleness on the part of the child. From the child's point of view, however, the use of 'and' to link sentences into one super-sentence is a triumph. What he begins to feel is that there are ways in which one sentence structure can be used, like an umbrella, to cover what would otherwise be more than one sentence. In other words, the use of 'and' is the child's response to the growing urge to achieve continuity and with it a sort of complexity in the structure of his sentences. When one comes to think of it, 'and' is really a very useful device. It enables long structures to be made out of short ones. And it lends itself very well to the expression of narratives:

> He got up out of bed and he went downstairs and he had his breakfast and he went out.

If the first goal of writing is to enable the reader to construe meaning with the minimum of bother, then this is a highly successful piece.

What happens next to the writer is that he begins to use 'and' for somewhat differentiated purposes to signal different sorts of meaning. Thus:

> He fell on his head and it hurt

suggests that the 'and' is used not just to link, which of course it does, but also to suggest some sort of explanation — that the hurting was caused by the falling.

His Mum got mad and smacked him

is another example. Close scrutiny of a child's writing may reveal many other instances. As a result, we can say that the use of 'and' is not quite as mindless as might have been supposed. It means rather different things at different times.

This last sentence shows another sort of advance. We have already mentioned that to achieve both coherence and cohesion in a piece is a major developmental aim. The same can be said about sentences themselves. Here we have two sentences

His Mum got mad.

and

His Mum smacked him.

They can be joined by what grammarians call coordination. Our sentence

His Mum got mad and smacked him

is an example of one sentence with two coordinated clauses.

He got up out of bed and he went downstairs and he had his breakfast and he went out

is another example of coordination — this time we have a sentence with four coordinated clauses.

Within such sentences as these it is possible to detect progression towards internal cohesion within the sentence. A major way in which this can be done is by a use of pronouns, by what is called pronominal reference. If we take the sentence

Tom got up and he went downstairs . . . ,

we find that some sort of internal unity is being achieved through the use of 'he' instead of Tom. Of course the word 'Tom' could have been repeated, but according to our conventions that would have seemed clumsy and so the child uses 'he', a pronoun, to refer to 'Tom' or, as he would probably put it, to 'stand for' Tom.

Pronominal reference is a very important device. As we shall see, it can be used between sentences as well as within them. It is not the only device which the child will soon hit upon. In fact, one of our sentences above already shows him to be using an alternative. The sentence

His Mum got mad and smacked him

is another example of a coordinated sentence, but here the child has used neither 'His Mum' nor the appropriate pronoun 'she' in the second clause. Instead, he has missed out any explicit mention of the subject within the clause and left us, quite legitimately, to carry through the meaning potential of 'His Mum' from the first clause. Thus within the coordinated structure we have interesting developments. The use of the word 'and' becomes differentiated. The child uses pronominal reference to bind coordinated clauses together and he uses elision (the missing out of all mention of the subject within the actual clause) which has the effect of binding the clauses together even more tightly.

In varying his coordinated sentences in this way the child is achieving cohesion within his sentence structure. He has also hit upon the use of important stylistic devices. What he has not yet learned fully are the limits to which these devices can be pushed. Imagine an adult producing a long coordinated sentence on the model

His Mum got mad and smacked him.

How long could one go on adding coordinated clause after coordinated clause and what would be the effect? Adults develop complex notions of taste, based largely upon what they themselves are used to meeting in print. So we can say that although the child has in a sense mastered these devices, he still has a long way to go before his mastery is anything like complete.

Some of the devices such as pronominal reference which he uses in connection with his production of coordinated sentences will stand him in good stead in the production of other types of sentence. It is to these, known as complex sentences, that we now turn.

A coordinated sentence has a sort of fulcrum, or more than one fulcrum, and the clauses on each side of that fulcrum carry equal grammatical weight. Such clauses are easily transformed into simple (one-clause) sentences. Thus

He fell on his head and it hurt

could easily become

He fell on his head

and

It hurt.

Of course, the movement towards complexity is in the opposite direction. We are suggesting that they could be split up only for the sake of illustration.

Because of the elision

His Mum got mad and smacked him

offers a slight difficulty. If we split up this sentence we should have to add either 'his Mum' or 'She' to the second sentence. Generally, the rule holds, though. Clauses that stand on either side of the fulcrum word in a coordinated sentence easily make sentences themselves. This is in contrast to the clauses in complex sentences. And so we can detect the difficulty a child will have in making complex sentences. It is that he simply cannot take two existing sentences and join them around a fulcrum word such as 'and'.

His problem is not to be solved merely by substituting some other sort of word for this fulcrum word (or coordinating conjunction, as the grammarians would call it). The first sort of complex sentence that most children use is one with a dependent clause of time — a 'when' clause. Take the sentence

He had his breakfast when he got up.

Here we have what counts as a complex sentence. If we try to split it into two or more simple sentences, we are in trouble.

He had his breakfast

seems to be satisfactory, but

When he got up

is not the sort of free-standing sentence that we could have expected to find if we have been transforming a coordinated sentence into its independent sentences.

This brings us to the heart of the matter. The coordinated sentence can be made by taking simple sentences and joining them, either with no alterations, other than those of punctuation and capitalisation, or with minimal alterations like the elision of the subject-word after its first mention. But when we try to make a complex sentence into more than one simple sentence, we have to take more radical measures.

It might be asked why a child should bother to move on to complex sentences, especially if coordination is working well for him. Basically, there are two answers. The first is that writing complex sentences helps the writer to avoid the monotony of that writing which is made up only of simple and coordinated sentences. The second has to do with meaning. Simple, co-ordinated and complex sentences are all structures which allow meanings to be communicated. But complex sentences allow meaningful relationships to be 'written down' in ways that would be found either difficult or impossible with other types of sentence. In fact the structures within the complex sentence are precisely for this purpose. Thus the 'when' clause of time allows a temporal or sequential relationship to be stated between two or more happenings. We can indicate a precise relationship by writing

When he was sixteen he got a job.

Although time relationships come first, other relationships, also mirrored in the clause structure, follow later. Thus cause and effect relationships are indicated with 'because . . . ' clauses, subtle conditions with 'if . . . ' clauses and so on.

Complex sentences, then, are a vital part of the writer's repertoire. Why are they so difficult to write? Or, if that is not obvious, why do they appear later than simple and coordinated sentences? The first answer is that they mirror complex relationships and those relationships have to be understood. In short, the mature development of complex clauses waits upon cognitive understandings. The second reason is that such understandings then have to be embodied in linguistic manipulations or understandings. If one is going to combine two sentences into a complex sentence, then one of the resultant clauses must be subordinate and one a main clause. The main clause would stand on its own feet in much the same way as we found each of the clauses in a coordinated sentence could become an independent sentence. The other clause, though, could do no such thing.

The picture we have given then is an idealised version of what happens. It is probably true that clauses can be used before they are properly understood. Elsewhere we give an example of a child using a 'because' clause without understanding its role in explaining cause and effect. And so the structure may appear before the cognitive development that is necessary to cope with its meanings has taken its full course. And it is probable that children do not actually combine two sentences but go straight for the creation of a complex sentence.

This leaves us to explain that the child still has the problem of recognising the status of what he has written. It may be that the child has reached the stage at which he aims to be writing sentences. How is he to agree that the complex sentence is in fact a sentence? If he is to allow it into his texts, it must pass some test and that must rest on an implicit understanding of the status of the dependent clause — that it is not itself a sentence, but that it is legitimate to have incorporated it into a certain sentence structure, one for which he might have no *name* but which we should call a complex sentence.

In summary, then, the child follows a line of development which involves him in using some of the resources he has brought from speech, whilst discarding others. The organisation of speech into information units carried by intonation patterns has, eventually, to be superseded. The dynamics of conversation have to be replaced by the creation of written texts which is essentially a solo operation. When the child gets beyond what a single simple sentence will convey, he has to take on, therefore, new problems of thematic coherence and of textual cohesion both within and between sentences. He has long been able to make sentences up but he has not distinguished them from other utterances. Now, the idea of what a sentence is grows. As it grows, it has to become more complicated. The child has to realise that this is a structure which, while helping to serve the purposes of communication, also contributes to coherence and cohesion. It is a structure which exists in three types, simple, compound or coordinate and complex. Each of these is capable of being elaborated and the last, in particular, may carry arrays of structural devices which assist in conveying certain relationships. Thus the notion of the sentence is a crucial one for the child. As we pointed out earlier, this notion is not one that is reached through listening to definitions, but as the result of the experience of reading, of trying to write and of discussing examples and non-examples with the teacher.

Texts have to be organised; the spontaneous and unpremeditated character of much talk is now a poor model for writing. The principle that seems to come most easily to children is the narrative which embodies some sort of chronological ordering. This may be one reason why the first subordinate clause in the first complex sentence that the child writes is likely to be a time clause, probably beginning with 'when'.

As time goes on children need more varied help in organising their writing. They need to write for different purposes because each purpose makes its own demands upon the grammar. For example, speculative writing might employ the conditional 'if . . . '. Instructions, on the other hand, might call upon the imperative: 'First do this . . . ' and so on. Then the child will need help in coming to terms with genres. Here the reading programme will assist. He will experience different sorts of writing such as articles, poems, notices, headlines and so on in his capacity as a reader, and the conferences with his teacher will give him the chance to discuss the attributes of genres in terms of their form and of the distinctive uses that each genre makes of language.

Finally, in his development as a writer, the child needs to become sophisticated about his own role. He will begin to see, as he goes through the junior years, that there is a changing role for him as planner of his own writing: that he can move from a crude sort of intention to mean to a more calculated and orderly planning of longer pieces. He will see that his job as a composer is to make meanings accessible to others — whom he might never see or hear — and to make cohesive texts in which the language is appropriate, and the subject matter or ideational content is coherent. He will do this by understanding and exploiting sentence structure. And as he does so, he will come to understand that language items always have several purposes — they have a potential for meaning, but at the same time they relate to one another in complex ways.

Understanding this is likely to lead to the notion that managing such complexity is not something that necessarily can be easily done or as the result of single tries. In this way, the idea of reviewing and eventually also of proofreading will develop.

The teacher's role in fostering writing

After this brief sketch of the ways in which the child's ability to write will develop, we now turn to the teacher in order to examine what she can do to foster this development. As we do so, we shall take the opportunity to fill out certain parts of the child's pattern of development in the hope that this will allow us to shed further light on the teacher's role. What the teacher can do ranges from the formal to the informal, from the direct to the indirect and from the global to the specific.

Understanding the developmental progression

It is the developmental progression that gives the teacher her broad aims. Her job is quite simply, to foster this progression. The sketch given above is a mere outline and lacks chronological precision, but within its limits it seems to be valid at least for those in a British culture whose first language is English. Because it is only a sketch, however, it glosses over some differences between individuals which may have significance. The most obvious differences between one child and another, though, seem to lie mainly in what each brings to the whole business of learning to write and then also in the speed at which progress is made.

Learning to write is not a matter of maturation, with growth coming mainly from within. On the contrary, according to the standpoint adopted in these pages, development is largely a matter of interaction and of soundly establishing the preceding stages of learning so that advances can then be made. Much of what it takes to become a successful writer does not come about as a result of 'learning to write' in any narrow sense but is based on much wider experiences of the environment as a whole, of people, of trying to communicate and to understand in spoken language and, not least, experience of written language delivered by a story reader, usually the parent or teacher, through the ear rather than through the eye.

Much of what follows in this section is intended to help teachers in their narrower and more highly focused concerns with writing. But the foundations of writing are laid over a long period of time, and very often even the 'remedial' actions necessary to advance a child's attainment may not lie in anything the teacher can do with a particular piece of writing in mind. Success in writing, we need to remember, depends on the curriculum as a whole, on life's experiences, and on the rest of the language work of the school.

The danger of overloading

Writing, we know, is always a complex business. What the writer actually has to do is very varied and this is true at all stages of development. As a child progresses, handwriting and spelling become more nearly automatic. He learns to routinise certain procedures such as ways of opening or closing particular sorts of writing and ways of sequencing and connecting. As matters become automatic or routine, the writer is freed to turn his attention to other features of a particular act of composition. No matter how skilled he has become, there will always be such matters, always aspects of the business that are never completely or ideally satisfactory. In this sense, we deal with skill that is open-ended as well as complex. In such circumstances it is important that the learner should not be discouraged by what may seem an unmanageable set of tasks. In one sense, there is, fortunately, a built-in protective device for like the horizon, goals recede as, and only as, advances are made.

Nevertheless, it is important that the teacher does not pitch her immediate aspirations impossibly high. We shall deal with this in more detail when we come to discuss both the setting of assignments and the devising of a marking policy. Here, we point out the twin dangers. The first is inherent in always seeing much further than the child — which ought to be the teacher's strength — and of setting goals that are beyond his reach. The second is linked to this. There is a limit to what any individual can process at any one time. Writing, as we have pointed out, requires the simultaneous processing of handwriting and layout data, spelling, the generation and ordering of content, and the selection of language items bearing in mind the needs to communicate and to create a true text in language that is appropriate and effective. In the earlier stages, the problems of handwriting and spelling may be foremost in the child's mind. If so, he will give them his main attention and the other problems of processing will receive less attention or be ignored altogether. In such circumstances it is necessary that the teacher should make no undue demands of the child that might overload his ability to manage such diverse matters. In other words, the teacher should look for visible progress mainly, and perhaps only, in those parts of the whole which are the child's immediate concern while gently seeing to it that those concerns do not remain static. It calls for considerable tact. As a rule, it will help to look for small-scale improvements in specific areas rather than global progress.

The use of spoken language

The young child's knowledge of language is gained through the ear and is, therefore, mainly of spoken language. We have already discussed the status of this knowledge as a major resource and we have also indicated its limitations. There is no doubt that the effectiveness of the writing programme will depend not only on the child's prior experience of spoken language but also on his making continuing advances in his listening and talking. Spoken language ought to be a growing resource. Advances build up a background knowledge which is essential in his career as a writer. Similar considerations apply to his more general knowledge of the world, whether it is gained through spoken language or not. Writers cannot do without such knowledge. Moreover, the pleasures and thrills involved in the process of acquiring it, as opposed to merely possessing it, can be a powerful stimulant in making the child want to find out more and also to communicate what he learns.

Progress in writing is influenced by other parts of the language policy work, too. For example, the child's knowledge of written language and of the uses to which it is put, of the styles in which it can be expressed and the genres into which it can be fashioned is enhanced through the reading programme. In this programme, it will be remembered, the teacher's reading aloud to the children played a prominent part.

Spoken language remains the major vehicle by means of which there is communication between teachers and between the child and other children about writing. The reading programme, it will be remembered, gave many opportunities for, and is itself furthered by the use of spoken language. In particular, styles and genres can be discussed. Such important matters as openings and endings, the introduction of characters, the setting of the stories, the changing of topics within a piece of writing can all be discussed with the child or with a group of children. Jerome Bruner has insisted that matters of great complexity can be discussed with children at a level that is appropriate for them. This is certainly true of such literary devices as would be identified in these discussions. Setting and character can be discussed quite as effectively with infants as with undergraduate students. Here, we should note the double purpose of such discussions. In the first place they should serve to educate the child in the ways that what he is reading, or what is being read to him, actually works. They should also add to his store of models and routines that he can utilise in his own writing whenever he feels that it would be appropriate to do so.

A further use for speech is in giving the child feedback about his writing. Feedback can be of different kinds. For example, there is the affective feedback which is often used. It might take the form of a comment at the end of a child's story; 'This was a lovely story, James. I did enjoy it,' or 'Very good,' or 'I am looking forward to reading your next story, Anne.' Such feedback serves the purpose of assuring the child (and anyone else who reads it) that the teacher is no ogre but is a warm human being, sympathetic, probably slow to anger and essentially lovable. Alas, it does little for the child who is actively experimenting with, perhaps, spellings, or formulaic openings, or with getting a character onto the page. It is suggested that such warbling should be replaced as soon as possible by comments that are appreciative of what the writer is actually struggling with and which give some indication of whether he has actually been successful. Of course, once a particular feature has been singled out and especially if he has been praised, the child is likely to move to excess, to overuse. If his use of a striking opening is identified and shown to be effective, we are quite likely to get a rash of similar openings. The same is true of his other efforts. A good and effective use of an adjective is likely to bring a surfeit of adjectives, or so it may seem from the adult's point of view. From the developmental point of view, however, the child is doing exactly what we would hope. He is experimenting to establish his skill more certainly and also enquiring to find the limits of the effectiveness of his 'new' ploy. Thus there is no need for the teacher to worry about such moves. Any excess will right itself in time. In the meantime, the teacher, once she understands what is going on, is in a position to help or to let the matter run its course without any further intervention on her part.

It is not only comments from the teacher and discussion between the teacher and the child that are valuable. It was suggested in Chapter 5 that there should be occasions when children read what other children have written. This element began with transitional reading and, it will be recalled, continued throughout the primary years. As time goes on, this reading can be supplemented by discussion in which the writer gets feedback from other children who have read his work. Such operations can only be successful when they are set up and controlled by a highly skilled teacher. Children can be perverse and dismissive in their comments and the giving of feedback requires some skill. Nevertheless, there are questions which can be answered by other children. Did they understand what was written? If not, could they be definite in indicating what they found difficult? Did they enjoy the story? If so, exactly what did they like? In such ways children can be encouraged not to be destructive and they can also be put on their mettle by the demand to be specific. And, of course, it is when feedback is specific that the writer is most likely to benefit from it.

Marking policy

Perhaps the best indicator of quality in the way in which a school manages children's writing (and possibly much else besides) is its attitudes to marking. There are schools where the head insists on the ritual marking of every 'error', perhaps so that he, and parents, can be assured that teachers are doing their jobs, paying diligent attention to what the children are doing and, at the same time, 'maintaining standards'. What lies beneath such a 'policy' shows a deep misunderstanding of what progression in writing is like and what the teacher's role should be. It misunderstands also what 'standards' really are and, not least, shows a deplorable attitude to parents.

Of all the time spent in planning a language policy, none is likely to be more profitable than that spent on discussing a policy for marking. The first thing to establish is that it is not the purpose of marking to draw the child's attention to every error that he makes or to every shortcoming that he shows. Still less is it to extirpate linguistic heresy with the teacher in the role of grand inquisitor, grimly examining the sins of the writer, perhaps before burning, or at least disfiguring, his works.

Marking has two main purposes. The first is to assess the attainment of the writer. In global terms this is quite difficult to do, especially if one is expected to quantify. There are no simple tests which do with writing what reading tests purport to do with reading. There is, of course, an even earlier question to answer before anyone goes to the trouble of assessing writing. It is 'Why bother?' one can suggest several plausible reasons. For example, someone might want to compare standards over a period of time to see whether there has been any advance or deterioration. The Assessment of

Performance Unit is struggling to devise instruments and techniques that might make this possible. To date, they do not impress with their results. A further reason might be to see whether a particular child has made progress over a period of time. As an extension, the same might be done with a class or group of children, perhaps with a view to deciding whether methods, resources and allocation of time were adequate. Such reasons all require a certain amount of precision in global assessment. Our present state of knowledge makes such precision impossible to attain; and it may be that such precision is in practice unattainable. General impressions are another matter. If one wants to know whether a child has made progress over a given time, the best way is to take examples of his work at each end of the period and compare them. Indeed, one would like to suggest that this should become common practice. The way to record a child's progress in writing is to keep a file of samples of his work, each dated and each with an accompanying commentary. If one then wants to go on to make general comments about groups of children, one can do so. But it is important to remember the somewhat intuitive and rather tenuous basis on which the comments are founded. And the summing of tenuous comments should, it goes without saying, be treated with some reserve.

The second and main reason for making judgements about a child's writing should be this: so that he can be helped to learn. This is the principle that should underlie a school's marking policy. If marking is going to help learning it should be seen as part of the process of giving feedback so that if comments are put upon a child's work, they become the basis for discussion. Such comments cannot be comprehensive. They cannot deal with every aspect of writing nor with every error that the child makes. On the whole they should be made with certain concerns in mind. These might include, for instance, the strengthening of the child in his use of some particular expression, stylistic device, organisational principle, vocabulary or whatever. There is what Vygotsky called the zone of potential learning — an area in which, and only in which, progress is possible — and it is in this zone that the teacher should operate when he is marking or otherwise giving feedback. On the whole such comment should aim at being positive rather than negative. In other words, letting a child know when he has been successful is the main consideration. Negative feedback should be softened; 'I see what you are trying to do. I don't think it quite works. Couldn't you . . . ?'

The point about such comments is that they are specific. The puzzle for teachers is what they should be specific about. That is why comments on a child's work tell the visitor a very great deal about the teacher and the school. They reveal, in fact, at least as much about the expertise of the teacher as they do about the ability of the child. Marking is only successful when it is aimed at helping the child with his problems, with both identifying them and solving them. And this can only be done when it is based on insights into the ways in which children learn and into what they learn — when it is based, in other words, on an understanding of progression.

Making a commentary

It was suggested above that the problem of record-keeping in relation to a child's writing might be solved by preserving samples of his writing together with a commentary on each. What might such a commentary actually be about?

In the first place it might be noted whether the child was in the transitional stage of literacy, had started to move out of that stage, or had arrived at autonomous reading and writing.

Then there might be indications about the purity of the written language and a note of any 'interference' from spoken language. For example, whether the child is still relying on a sort of phantom intonation to get the meaning across.

The child's mastery of sentence form might come next. There are several questions to be answered here. For example does he normally write in sentences? Are the sentences coherent in themselves? Is the child writing compound (that is, coordinated) sentences? Have complex sentences made an appearance? If so, has the child gone beyond using only 'when' clauses? Does he yet use other than time clauses?

Is there coherence not just within sentences but also in successions of sentences? In other words, is the subject matter handled in an ordered way? Is there cohesion? Does the language flow without jerks and breaks from one sentence to another? Is the child developing, as he should already have done with sentences an *idea* of what a paragraph is? Does the child give evidence of wishing not merely to express himself but to communicate successfully?

Does the child appear to be extending his self-concept as a writer? Does he give any sign of planning what he has written, of revising it, or of spontaneously doing more than one draft — especially if the writing is not 'private' and is for circulation or publication?

Setting writing tasks

Although the teacher must take ultimate responsibility for what the child writes, there is much to be said for allowing children to pursue their own interests and wishes wherever possible. If a child wants to write a story or an article or to follow some investigations which might result in a report, he should be allowed to do so unless there is a good reason to the contrary. In a class which has a buoyant atmosphere children not only want to learn, they will often identify what it is that they want to learn. One of the problems of the school whose atmosphere is dismal is in motivating the children. The buoyant school has solved this in a general way. Therefore it would be wise for the teachers to allow and even to urge children to determine and to follow their own paths, at least for some of the time.

Of course, there are limits set by the length of the day and by the wish to meet other needs, so there must be balance in the long run. Given such limitations, can we ask how much writing there ought to be or, alternatively, how much time a child should spend on writing tasks?

Writing shares a characteristic with the other language skills that some may find surprising. No-one has any idea of how much practice is needed to attain proficiency. This is partly because such skills are all open-ended, they draw on so much else, as we have repeatedly pointed out — and this is quite separate from differences in the individual potential of children.

Accordingly, it is not possible to say that in the interests of gaining certain 'standards' so much time ought to be devoted to these skills including writing. At present there seems to me to be far too much writing and much of what there is seems to be quite pointless. Jokes abound in school among children who, having been taken to inspect the windmill, then say 'Have we got to write about it, Miss?' Unfortunately, writing is the teacher's fall-back. While it is being done, children are in a heads-down posture. When it is finished there is a visible product for all to see — in contrast to the outcomes of speech which is transient.

Nevertheless with all these 'advantages' there are strong reasons for feeling disquiet about situations where writing is seen, mindlessly, as an inevitable outcome. In the first place, writing may not be appropriate to the learning that it is hoped may take place. Speech, and particularly discussion, might often serve the purpose better. The safe rule from the point of view of good attitudes to writing is this: do not ask children to write if there is a better way of achieving learning ends.

These reasons are not superficial for they go deep into the heart of what it is that we do when we write. A sense of engagement in writing is crucial. It determines whether a child wants to write or, indeed, whether he will write. Both how much he writes and the quality of what he writes also depend very much on this sense of engagement. It is a form of motivation.

Engagement goes even further because it leads directly into an intention to mean and to communicate. When this intention is established, remarkable things begin to happen. There needs to be a clear and persistent impulse if the topic of the writing is to be developed coherently, if appropriate structures are to be found, if felicitous phrasing is to be achieved, if there is to be cohesion in the development of the text and if there is to be a judgement about the degree of explicitness necessary in order to communicate with the readers.

It is, consequently, very important to the writing task that the reader should feel this sense of engagement with writing as a process. Writing has phases in which a number of matters is pursued simultaneously. It needs to be informed by a purpose and that purpose must be strong enough to allow the writer to sense the effects on, and implications for, other phases, of whatever he decides to do in a particular phase. The purpose that carries this burden throughout is the intention to mean. Unless it is strong, the writing task is unlikely to be successful and may even be counterproductive. If this intention to mean is not always present, then there are probably too many writing tasks facing the child.

With this severe limitation in mind, we must now point in the other direction. Within writing as a whole there are many genres — types of writing with their own distinctive styles, physical layout and overall purposes — letters, plays, articles, novels, short stories, poems, and so on — and each genre can usually be divided into subcategories. As well as genres there are purposes, some of which determine which genre shall be inhabited. Thus there is writing to inform, to persuade, to record and so on. The importance of drawing such distinctions as genre and purpose is this: there do seem to be skills of writing which can be used over wide ranges of genres and for different purposes, but each genre also has its own distinctive language uses and the same can be said about purpose. The point is that a general writing competence is not to be achieved by writing in one, or even in several genres, or for single purposes. Competence across the board involves practising in different genres and writing for many different purposes.

There is another reason why this is so. Even if a genre employs resources that have been learned and used elsewhere, what makes a genre identifiable is that its *use* of such resources is distinctive. In other words, it is the putting together that counts. Using new resources and putting together old resources in ways that acknowledge the various needs of genre and purpose are basic reasons for extending the range of the child's writing.

In learning about genre and purpose it might be useful if the child were acquainted with an initial three-part division, each part carrying its own implications for the writer. This division is into writing for

(1) expression
(2) recording
(3) communication.

The benefits of the first are exclusively for the writer; indeed, it may be that no-one else will read it. The second — writing to record — immediately raises the question: why do you want a record? In other words, it takes the issue of purpose a little further. This, incidentally, is an important part of the study skills with which we shall deal more fully in Chapter 7 . The main requirement is that records should both include all the information which is *essential for the purpose in hand* and also be intelligible to the person for whom they are intended — usually the writer himself. There is a third requirement that the record should be as economical as possible in the circumstances. The third category, communication, overlaps with the others but is mainly concerned with the communication of meanings to other people. When this becomes important, it requires that the writer shall have learned from his reactions to his own and to other people's writing and from the reactions of others through the comments they have made on his own writing. From this he develops a generalised sense of audience, a sense of what will and will not be understood, of what will and will not amuse or intrigue others, and so on. This is a major part of his learning. Unless the child is successful, he is unlikely ever to be, or to feel himself to be, a successful writer. It is the core of communicative competence.

From this point, the child can be encouraged to venture into wider fields. He needs the practice but what he needs even more than practice is a sense of engagement and an intention to mean. Unless these operate as strong and pervasive influences, he will not get far; nor should the teacher expect him to.

We turn now to examine some other aspects of progression. Given 'engagement' on the part of the child, what is it that makes one writing task more difficult than another? The question is a hard one and would require an extensive answer. Here we can point out two aspects of the problem. There is, first, the match between whatever linguistic ability is needed to perform a task successfully and the child's own linguistic abilities or, in some cases, the child's perception of his own linguistic abilities. Here feedback can help in showing a child what he can actually do. Understanding the results of what one has tried to do is always important and this is one of the insights that feedback can bring. With this rather important qualification that it is the child's perception of his own abilities that is just as important as any other measure or estimate of them, it remains true that the tasks set must be capable of being done at whatever linguistic level the child operates.

However, linguistic ability is always enmeshed in other sorts of ability. Tasks need also to be suited to the child's cognitive skills. Here the danger is more of a mismatch that underestimates the child. Much topic work, for example, is pitched at a level that is too low. Very often the level is one of merely collecting and expressing information and concepts. Of course, there is nothing wrong with information and concepts but they represent something near the bottom line in a hierarchy of cognitive skills and the child needs also to work at higher and more involved levels.

Writing conferences

There is much to be said for an arrangement in which teacher and child meet privately to discuss matters connected with the child's writing ability, just as there is a place for similar conferences to deal with his reading. In earlier sections of this chapter there have been suggestions that could be taken up in such conferences. Giving feedback is by far the most important of these. There are others such as getting the child to understand his developing role as a writer. Ways of planning, revising and proofreading will then be accepted as part of this developing role. Establishing the idea of a sentence as a set of structures which can be expanded through co-ordination, through subordination (that is, through the writing of complex sentences), or by elaboration and expansion at key points, is another priority.

What the child will also find very helpful is to discuss writing tasks before he attempts them. The teacher can lead the child into identifying problems of control and organisation, and together they can discuss possible solutions. The teacher might also suggest key words, while taking care not to circumscribe too narrowly the child's own thinking.

Collaborative writing might also be attempted with the child and teacher as joint authors. Joint authorship gives excellent opportunities to identify and solve problems — 'How are we going to begin?', 'How are we going to introduce such a character?', 'How shall we end?', 'Do you think we could find a way of fitting what we want to say in this part of the sentence?', 'Don't you think that that seems a bit odd? Can't we find a better way to write it?' Questions such as these, levelled in the course of writing, may have a profound effect on the child, for while they seem to be about the writing of a particular piece, they are also about the business of composing in general. There is no doubt that some children can gain enormously from such collaboration. Collaborative writing (with the result published jointly) provides the most promising chance of learning insights in rather the same way as apprentices learn from master craftsmen.

Group and class activities

As children progress, there are several activities which might help them to make their skills more secure and to advance them further. One such activity has been suggested in connection with the reading programme. It was referred to as group sequencing. What it encourages children to do is to restore sections of a text, which have been artificially put into random order by the teacher, back into their right order. It was suggested that each proposal made by the children should always be accompanied by reasons. Such activity gives insight into the structure of texts and into the thematic and cohesive devices that writers can use to weld the whole together.

Another activity which can be attempted by a group is to take a passage from which all punctuation marks have been removed and repunctuate it. Again, the resulting discussion may help children to understand the use of orthographic markers and also of the structures that they mark.

A further suggestion is to take a simple sentence with a subject and a predicate and then to work at elaborating each. What the children may come to understand is that there are, in effect, slots in sentences into which other language can be fitted if it suits the writer's purpose. Thus in the sentence

The dog barked,

we can take the subject and, if we wish, pack more information-bearing structures around it. In the slot before the headword, 'dog' we might put 'black' or 'big black', and after 'dog' we might put 'which was big and black'. Discussing the relative advantages of each strategy might be useful, for it gets into matters of style, purpose and felicitous phrasing. With the predicate there are potentially many more slots. Once such slots have been identified and filled, children can be encouraged to search for similar examples in their own reading. By such means they get 'on the inside' of structures.

All these activities are essentially 'garage' activities, while both reading and writing are really 'open road' activities. It is essential that garage work should never be more than a small proportion of the whole. Real contexts and real meanings are of the essence and the subtleties of dealing with them are far greater than the most ingenious deviser of exercises can ever allow. Also, motivation must be kept high. Engagement and the intention to mean, I repeat, are indispensable attributes of anyone who wishes to learn to write.

This is why language textbooks are self-defeating. There can be no place for them in the development of writing, and in a properly conducted school there would be no time to use them. The open road beckons and with it goes high morale and real, purposeful motivation. It would be a pity ever to confine children and to condemn them to artificiality and drabness, simply because of the apparent convenience of such books.

7

Language in Learning and Across the Curriculum

This chapter is divided into two main sections. Section 1 deals with the role of language in learning, and section 2 deals with study skills. To some extent the second section is an application of the first but it ranges more widely and deals with such matters as attitudes to study, the role of discussion in study and nature and status of knowledge itself.

Section 1: the role of language in learning

There are several controversial questions which pertain to the relationship between language and learning and between linguistic development and cognitive development. Perhaps the most important of them has to do with the problem of primacy, with the answer to the question: which comes first, linguistic development or cognitive development? Is it the case that language determines thought, as Benjamin Lee Whorf argued? I believe that it is possible to give a clear answer but that the question is misconceived, or rather that it is not as important as it once was thought to be. I do not believe that it is desirable to take a narrow (and, therefore, I would argue, a simplistic view) of the way in which language is used in other learning. Indeed, a basic theme that runs through this chapter is that a great deal of other learning is necessary to the development of linguistic competence and that linguistic competence, which itself includes and makes use of these other sorts of learning, is then used in the pursuit of further learning. What we know when we know language is always, I shall argue, an amalgam of the linguistic and other sorts of knowledge. What results from all this is, therefore, a cumulative or spiralling process. I should add that, in exploring the implications of this idea, I have come to entertain the possibility that rigidly to distinguish the linguistic from the non-linguistic may lead to serious error; that many of the distinctions such as that which separates the linguistic from, say, the cognitive, which many of us picked up early in our professional training, may be seriously misleading. It follows, of course, that a broad and inclusive view of linguistic development such as I demand will have implications for study skills as these are a kind of application of linguistic knowledge. Accordingly, in section two, I shall put forward the idea that the narrow view of study skills which, it seems to me, is extant in schools is not a useful one, and may be destructive of our efforts to help children to learn. Much of section two is given to a redescription of study skills and to a brief account of their uses.

In this section I shall discuss certain matters which seem to me to bear on the questions of language and learning. I shall look first at the relationship between language and learning and particularly at the primacy controversy. In doing so I shall use the work of the Swiss, Jean Piaget, and the American, Benjamin Lee Whorf, to establish my bearings and set my course. Then I shall identify some early learning which is not at all linguistic, as well as some that is. Much of this learning, including some of the non-linguistic learning, I shall argue, is incorporated into subsequent language learning.

As in all matters to do with the development of children we soon run up against the constraints set by Piagetian doctrine which is clear on the primacy question. However, I think that the evidence against Piaget is now so strong and convincing that we need no longer feel bound to orthodoxy and the way is open for us to seek a more convincing account of the relationships between language and learning. More radically still, once the Piagetian paradigm is brought under scrutiny, we need to ask whether it is possible to go further and to question the whole categorial basis of our thinking and investigations. Is it time, for example, to begin to treat the old divisions into 'cognitive', 'linguistic', 'social' and so on as quite implausible divisions, shored up by historical accident and buttressed by the division of labour, particularly among psychologists?

The position that I take is that both Whorf and Piaget offer valuable and useful insights but that both are wrong in their conclusions. Although the conclusions that I offer are very significantly different from both of theirs, I owe a debt to both.

Linguistic primacy and beyond

The connections between language and thought are of the utmost importance. To state it at the outset, my view is that language has a vital, but not exclusive, role in both thinking and learning. More precisely, I belong with those who would assign to it a crucial role in infancy, during the school years and beyond, and I believe that this role needs to be properly understood so that education in school can be conducted on sure foundations.

We can approach the question of primacy through the two theorists and investigators, Piaget and Whorf, who have been interpreted as putting forth diametrically opposite views. Piaget has been regarded as the classic proponent of the doctrine that the child's linguistic development awaits prior cognitive development. Whorf, on the other hand, has been seen as the principal protagonist of the doctrine of what has been called 'linguistic relativity'. Briefly, this holds that thought and thinking are different in each culture in the world and that the principal determinant of such differences is language. Thus when languages have a close familial relationship, as do, for example, those of western Europe, so in turn do thought and thinking. Hence, in seeking to point to differences between the West and American Indians, Whorf looked to the language as the source of those differences.

A scrutiny of both Whorf and Piaget shows a more complex picture than that of mere opposition. In the first place, my placing of the two as opposites is somewhat artificial. Although they took very different stances, they did not engage in argument with each other. And so, neither was concerned to appraise or to try to qualify the work of the other in any significant way.

Piaget certainly insisted that it was cognitive development and perhaps also a more general semiotic development, too, which made language possible. But once a certain cognitive stage was reached, the role of language changed and by the time of formal operations — near or during adolescence — language played a significant part in certain cognitive operations and thus in the further development of the individual. Whorf stressed that the underlying metaphysical assumptions of a culture were enshrined in its language — notions of being, becoming, existing and of time, for example, and that these underlay thinking. Moreover, it was through lexical and grammatical relationships that these assumptions manifested themselves so that when a speaker was inducted into a language he was also inducted into ways of thinking and of regarding the world. But

133

Whorf did not adequately explain how language came about in the first place. Of course, if all thinking were really linguistically determined and if this were true in historical as well as in individual development if, that is, language played a phylogenetic as well as an ontogenetic role, then the question must be raised of how in the primitive absence of language there could be thought at all. To restate it, my own position is that what Piaget averred to be true only of the stage of formal operations, namely that linguistic development formatively contributes to cognitive development, is more generally true.

Part of the controversy is easily resolved. The strict question of primacy is soon settled. If we ask which comes first, language or cognition, the answer is plainly that cognitive development precedes linguistic development. Infants can quite obviously perform a variety of cognitive operations, some of them immensely sophisticated, before they can, in any sense, use natural language. These operations include various kinds of thinking and learning. And so, what I should call the 'totalist' view, which holds that thinking as such is impossible without language, fails. This is the 'hard' version of the theory of linguistic determinism. It is also clear that thinking takes place in other species which do not seem to have natural language at all, but this is indicative rather than conclusive, for human beings might be exceptional in this respect. It could still be the case that they, alone and in contrast to other species, cannot think or learn without language. However, it is so well-established that thinking and learning take place before the onset of language that the 'hard' hypothesis is completely invalidated. Deaf children, too, learn and think without natural language, though it is just possible that they invent a private and personal language-substitute or symbol system for such purposes. Further, it is also likely that certain sorts of learning and thinking, which go on in children after the acquisition of language, are not dependent upon language. These, incidentally, are by no means restricted to the area of psychomotor activity which often seems remote or free from language.

Together, such considerations add up to a conclusive case: cognitive development precedes linguistic development in absolute terms; and further, some cognitive development goes on side-by-side with linguistic development, without necessarily involving language at all. But if we reformulate the question and ask whether there are vital links between language, on the one hand, and thinking and learning, on the other, whether, for example, it is the case that some thinking may be impossible without language (one has in mind those chains of reasoning which seem to be essentially verbal) and whether other kinds of thinking are more likely than not to be carried on with the aid of language, we must say, in all these instances that the answer is 'yes'.

Thus, to deny the exclusivity of language as the determinant of thinking is not to deny its potency. In a sense, the question of primacy matters little, for the real question with which we must engage, is not which comes first, but in what ways are thinking and learning permeated by language, and how is language learning affected or facilitated by other sorts of learning.

Early learning

It is important to emphasise the amount, the scope and the sheer earliness of learning that takes place before the onset of language. The starkly dramatic quality of what the psychologist, William James, called the great booming buzz of confusion that meets the newborn child turns out to be the result of an oversimplification. The picture that we can now see is not so much that of an organism trying to make sense — any kind of sense — of the world, as of an already active child, remembering, discriminating, already a superb intellectual/social learner. Such a child engages in many kinds of cognitive enterprise before he can talk and before he can understand language. It may be that his lack of muscular control, especially over his head and neck and over his defaecatory functions, together with his general physical helplessness, has been taken as indexical — just as it might be with those suspected of mental handicap or of advanced senility. But it is all too easy to underestimate what a child can do if we are influenced unduly by what he cannot do. In the cognitive world, and especially, perhaps, in the interpersonal world, the neonate makes advances with great rapidity. Moreover, he does so from learning that he has already effected as a prenate, for there is now clear evidence that cognitive activity of a quite impressive kind goes on while the child is still in the womb.

On reflection, this is not so surprising: it is just that received wisdom has got in the way of understanding. As ways of monitoring the physiological correlates, such as the heart-beat rate, have been developed and applied to the prenatal child, it has become apparent that he reacts to changes in sound level and temperature.

But a further discovery is particularly significant in several respects. It is now established that infants who have not heard their mother's voice since birth can nevertheless discriminate that voice when it is in competition with other women's voices saying more or less the same thing. It seems difficult to overstate the importance of this ability. It goes much further than the gross ability to be affected by sound level for it shows a capacity to fine-tune, to discriminate the voice from other sounds and, more delicately, to distinguish one voice from another on the basis of memories stored, that is of learning effected, before birth. If one is looking for the real roots of self-awareness, the ability to discriminate self from others, it is very possible that they may lie here. The phenomenon augurs well for the future success of language learning. Perhaps, as time goes on, we should even abandon our dating of children from their birthdays, in favour of an alternative which takes account of this early learning.

Leaving such fancies behind, we can insist that the extent of learning which is now attributed to very young children must cause us to review our estimation both of their abilities and of their potentialities. Two considerations, at least, are important. First, it is the case that learning is established earlier than was thought possible. Secondly, we are left with a strong suspicion that historically we may have been underestimating the knowledge and abilities of children, not just in their earliest days but perhaps throughout life as well, because this knowledge and these abilities are the foundations of later learning. This is different from, but related to, the commonsense notion that both general observation and introspection suggest that human beings are seriously underdeveloped in some important respects. Many of us feel that we have potential — in maths or in music, perhaps — which has not been developed to the full and which may, indeed, have been grossly stunted and impaired as early learning went wrong or perhaps because of neglect. As a result, we are entitled to the speculation, to put it no higher, that the intentions and aims of our child-rearing and schooling may not now be realistic and may be pitched far too low.

Recent discoveries all point in one direction: they give more and higher instances of ability and potential in very young children. What are we to make, for example, of J.B. Watson's discovery that a newborn child can remove an irritant from his nose with his hand and one from his leg by using the other leg? Tom Bower found that such children turn quickly away from smells they find unpleasant. They will also turn towards a pad soaked in their mother's milk in preference to one soaked in the milk of another mother. Wertheimer found that a few moments after birth children would look in the direction of a sound — a reaction which, it is known, depends on the difference in time that it takes the sound to arrive at each ear in turn. Newborns also exhibit a defensive response to an object moving closer to their eyes. Not all these phenomena can be explained by 'simple' reflex theory and so we must look towards more complex explanations. Still more remarkable is the fact that very young children, when face-to-face with their mothers, will imitate their facial movements consistently. Thus, when the mother flutters an eyelid, the child does the same. When she puts out her tongue, so does the child. When she opens her mouth wide, the child follows suit.

Such abilities as these may seem to be trivial but in reality they give remarkable clues to the immense psychological power of newborn children to use perceptual and other abilities that once would have been considered to develop much later. If ever they had been confronted by a buzzing world of confusion, they have soon brought it to order, for the act of perception is not just that of registering a sensation. It is always an act of classifying, of ordering, of discriminating and thus of understanding, in however elementary a way, that the world exists, that it has stable or recurrent features and that these can be recognised. Unless we posit that these abilities are all, so to speak, no more than evidence of early systems which see the child into his first days of separate existence and then die out, we must allow that here is the basis for the future development of more advanced abilities — for example, those involved in the development of such logical criteria as will be used in understanding conversation. Already, we have rudimentary inferencing, as when the child turns away from the unpleasant and towards the pleasant, or when he tries to avoid an approaching object. And, however it is to be understood, the power of first perceiving and then of imitating his mother's facial movements is an amazing example of virtuosity. It seems to show an ability not just to distinguish between self and an other, but also to identify similarities between the self and the other, together with the competence to single out quite complex motor responses and to operate them at will. Founded on the ability to pay attention to an other, this capability of responding to another's actions also takes us well into the domain of interpersonal or social behaviour.

The Piagetian constraint

With these and other discoveries in mind, it seems opportune to pose certain questions of a quite fundamental kind and to offer, somewhat speculatively on the basis of fact and 'best hunch', alternatives to some of the answers which are now commonly assumed to be correct.

If we ask about the stimulus and the setting for the most complicated of these early behaviours, it is clear that they are usually interpersonal. From these studies and from studies of older children (for example, those of Donaldson and her associates) estimates both of the level of a child's interpersonal skills and of the dating of his entry into the social world, shared in some sense by its inhabitants and felt to be common to them, need to be revised. Whatever new understandings emerge are likely to be important, both for their own sakes, and also because they have considerable consequences for our own subsequent understanding of the development of language.

I believe that the hardest part of understanding the social world — and it is also hard at the level of the mature adult — lies beyond the appreciation of its commonality in the realisation that it is different to each participant. It seems to me, as a speculation, that there may be two roots out of which such understanding grows. One is the appreciation that a physical scene is different when perceived from different standpoints. Piaget did some interesting investigations in this area, and his views, which stressed the severely circumscribed nature of children's understanding, have come to be, for the time being, received wisdom. I am sure that the time has come for a radical revision.

Piaget's investigations suffer, from my point of view, from two disabling characteristics. The first is his adherence to stage theory and his too vivid demarcation of one stage from another. His emphasis on the qualitative obscured other sorts of learning. His original hunch about the successive stages of intelligence in the infant and child seemed to be confirmed by his enquiries. Once confirmed, it hardened and changed its status from something like that of a hypothesis to that of a dogma.

This is what Thomas Kuhn in his book *The Structure of Scientific Revolutions* claims is typical of 'normal' science; it is the way in which science manages itself until it comes up against a brick wall. Then, as Kuhn tells us, the role of the scientists and of their associates in and around the scientific community becomes extremely interesting. Instead of behaving in the rational, judicious, speculative, sceptical, tentative and essentially open-minded way that is often associated with their professions, they behave in one of two ways. They either dig in, adopt extraordinary defences and ignore awkward cases, or else they assume that in principle such awkwardnesses are bound to be explained eventually within the bounds of their existing thinking. This is the point, I believe, at which the Piagetian school has now arrived. Although no psychologist has done more to foster interest than Piaget, and although we are all greatly in his debt, we must nevertheless now move to modify his stage theory to take account of new discoveries.

Some of the ways in which the Piagetian paradigm needs to be changed may become clearer after we take a look at the second characteristic which I believe to have vitiated his work: his estimation of the role of language. Other investigators have taken exception to Piaget because he seemed to confound their understandings about language, the way it developed and its connections with cognitive development. His position was quite unequivocal. Language development waited upon cognitive development and was itself determined by it. In other words, cognitive development was a necessary but not necessarily a sufficient condition of linguistic development. He did not actually spell out what the other conditions might be, beyond the development of a general semiotic and symbolising ability which was itself also dependent on cognitive development.

Among his antagonists were the associationists who held the field before him and whose views he swept aside. Elsewhere, the tenor of Russian psychology — neurologically oriented and very much concerned with signal systems — went far beyond the limits of understanding set by western associationism. The work of Vygotsky, his pupil, Luria, and their colleagues seemed to show that intellectual development became different in kind after the onset of language. Piaget himself was able to allow an important role to language in this respect, but only at the reflexive stage of formal operations — roughly at adolescence — and he denied its importance in earlier stages. Thus, there are two views, both agreeing that language is important. The Russians gave it this status at the beginning of childhood and Piaget at the end. My own view is close to that of the Russians and closer still to that of Bruner who sees language as extending and amplifying both cognition and cognitive development. I should be inclined to put it more strongly than he did and to stress that language transforms cognition and cognitive development and that this is something which must be understood to happen in a social and cultural context. Language has the ability to amplify, to extend, to itensify, and to particularise cognition: it opens the ways to new understandings which are not necessarily either logical or concerned with the properties of the physical world as the understandings with which Piaget typically concerned himself were. Instead, they belong with the personal, the interpersonal and with understandings that are operational rather than strictly logical. When we take this and add it to what we know of the ways in which language is learned, the two together seem to leave Piagetian stage theory far behind.

Models for observing and investigating

Before we can develop the argument further, we must look at another piece of theoretical apparatus which, while once useful, now only has limited value and that only when it is used with caution. This apparatus is a kind of model but it lacks the empirical and clinical backing which Piaget gave to his, and it has no claim to elegance, comprehensiveness or to rigour. Indeed, it is little more than a set of assumptions. Its defects and deficiencies are so obvious that many would want to deny its validity, its relevance to them, and some even doubt its existence. I refer to a device which is often used in teacher training as a mnemonic. It may take various forms, but a typical one would be what we might call the 'PILES' model. Although its theoretical standing may be in doubt, there is in contrast no room for doubt about its potency in practice.

One problem that the trainer of teachers and nursery nurses has is that of extending the perceptions of his students. When they (or anyone else) observe they do not merely use their eyesight. They see in the light of what they know. Thus there is a difference between what the football fan 'sees' at a match and what the uninformed attender 'sees'. A builder does not see a house in the same way as the rest of us do and a joiner sees a piece of timber in his own way. And so, in order to extend the observational powers of students, the 'PILES' model was developed. In effect, its purpose was to remind students that when they are looking at children and when they are considering child development, it might be useful for them to think in terms of such headings as 'Physical', 'Intellectual', 'Linguistic', 'Emotional', and 'Social'. And the ploy has worked. It has given students some idea what they should look for;

it has helped to extend their somewhat primitive and global notion of 'development'. So far, so good. But it is well-established among more sophisticated model users that models, while they may be both useful and potent, are nevertheless temporary, tentative and sometimes even disreputable devices. The 'PILES' model is no exception. It seems to reduce both the development of children and the understanding of students to five separate dimensions. It ignores the question of whether there might not be others. It contains ambiguities which remain as long as the model is one of no more than crude headings. What, we might ask, is 'Physical'? Does it mean skeletal or psychomotor, or both? What is 'Intellectual'? Is it the same as 'cognitive'? What does 'Emotional' mean? What are the boundaries of the 'Social'?

Further, the categories are not mutually exclusive. Is there not overlap between the emotional and the social and between the intellectual and the physical? Could not certain phenomena be accommodated as easily under one heading as they could under another? Does not the 'social' depend on cognitive perceptions of people, their appearance, what they say and what they do? My present concern is, of course, mainly with the possible links between the linguistic and the intellectual. At a simple level one must deny that the two can ever be firmly separated, except perhaps temporarily for the purposes of discussion. If perception is part of the intellectual process, then listening and reading are at that level intellectual as well as linguistic. At a deeper level, too, when one is concerned with understanding language and with meaning, such states or processes are quite as much intellectual as they are linguistic.

If we were operating in psychology with some sort of faculty model — holding that there are parts of the mind which, working more or less separately, each deals with such diverse matters as emotion, interpersonal matters, understanding of the physical world, language and so on — there might be some sense in keeping and using the PILES model. Or, if it were used only as it was intended to be used in the first place — as a mnemonic for beginning students — it might be more easily defensible. Unfortunately, the model is a surface manifestation of something which strikes much more deeply — right into the division of labour among psychologists and other scholars. There are cognitive psychologists and there are social psychologists, not to mention psychotherapists and psychiatrists, each with distinctive concerns. In principle the division of labour has much to commend it. There is too much for individuals to learn and too much to understand unless the work can be split up in some way. Problems come when such divisions take upon themselves the attributes of completely separate disciplines. They attract their own communities of scholars. They develop their own journals. They establish their own fashionable concerns. They develop their own methods. They occupy their own departments in universities and mark out their own territories. The scholars in each set tend to share the same concerns, the same background theories and assumptions, the same paradigms as others in the same set. Because of specialisation they are able to work in great detail with the result that their work may then become quite inaccessible even to their near neighbours. And so, just as we have the divisions of the PILES model at the initial stages, so we have somewhat analogous divisions at the level of the academic and clinical expert. It is true that individuals sometimes try to bridge the gaps, but the divisions are often ill-defined and their different assumptions are hard to reconcile precisely because they are unstated and therefore unexamined. It is true that new disciplines may develop — such as psycholinguistics, which tries to occupy ground between, as well as ground common to, other disciplines. But to bridge gaps is easier said than done, partly because practitioners may not be reflexive enough about their own disciplines so that the import of what is being attempted is not always understood in its wider context, and partly because other relevant matter may still be ignored. For example, if they were to be faced with the speculation that language learning may be mainly a matter of interpersonal relations, or perhaps of the development of intersubjectivity, many psycholinguists might not be well equipped to deal with it. Even though the speculation is perfectly plausible, it would nevertheless be 'foreign' to most of them.

For teachers of children, the consequences are grave indeed. The seeming inability of scholars to put their own houses in order — and my plea here is not for unanimity and uniformity so much as for mutual and deep understanding — is discouraging and disabling to those whose task it should be to apply, albeit in a reflexive and critical way, certain insights derived from scholarly work. Of course, the teacher's task depends on more than what psychologists have to offer her. She needs also insights from elsewhere, from artists, from literature, from her own experience. But what comes from psychology and linked fields is essential. Without it, she cannot understand that development of the child as a learner and as a person that it is her aim to foster.

Teachers, then, are in danger of being left high and dry by the inadequacy of the theory that is available to them. They thus take on board the inadequate and partial. Or they may operate some kind of folk-psychology compounded of truths, assumptions, half-truths and incompatibles. I should like to suggest that there is to hand a compass by which to steer away from these treacherous waters. It is the realisation that, notwithstanding the implications of naive models and the limitations imposed by historical divisions of labour, the relationship between language and cognition is a two-way process. Even if we allow that language extends and transforms certain cognitive processes and in doing so radically affects cognitive development itself, we need to recognise that the use of language is itself dependent on understandings that are mainly cognitive in nature and which themselves are not in the traditional sense 'linguistic'. Given the basic account of language that has been offered in this book, this should not be surprising. Among the most significant features of language, as I see it, is its relationship to contexts and situations. It is from the larger cultural environment, the situation in which language is used, as well as from the narrower linguistic context that we must draw if we are to understand what language 'means'. This always entails understanding matters which are as wide as life's experience itself, which are not directly linguistic and which are not well illuminated by old models such as PILES or by the traditional separations of scholars and especially of psychologists.

Language and society

Much of the force and the general usefulness of language come from its interpersonal uses. Communication through language allows and even entails the transmission of information, attitudes, understandings and so on. In this way language becomes more than a vehicle or a medium which conveys content that has been, so to speak, 'thought of' and then enshrined in language. Language is itself the repository of attitudes and information. They are part of language and inevitably so. In this sense, the medium is part of the message.

Convention and meaning

In an earlier chapter, I was concerned to deny that language is meaningful in the way that it is generally taken to be. Meaning, as such, I held, was not in the word, nor in the grammar, nor in the intonation patterns, nor in any combination of these. It was in the mind or it was nowhere. Of course, the commonsense view is that language 'contains' meaning. In everyday life we all may ask for the meaning of a word. But this is a mistake. What language has, as Michael Halliday pointed out, is 'meaning potential'. Any stretch of language has potential, rather than actual meaning, and it is this potential that the individual who receives language processes into meaning. It is this same potential that the producer of language takes into account when he speaks or writes. This meaning potential is highly conventional and thus social. To say this is not to imply that all users are automatically fully aware of it, or that they sign some sort of social contract before being allowed to use language. What it does mean is that when, as members of society, they undergo the process of being socialised, they are inevitably inducted into language use and therefore into potential meanings.

In this sense, language users are inheritors of vast systems. These systems go far beyond the systems which, in my earlier analysis, I said were intrinsically part of language — the lexis, the grammar and the phonological patterns. They include principles extant in the cultural which govern what may be spoken about and when, and in what way it may be spoken about. For example, some subjects are taboo; other subjects are to be treated with reticence. Conversations, as a result, do not normally swing (at least in my subculture) to matters of income level or to sexual practices, though they might do so in special circumstances. The rules which govern all this are rarely made fully explicit. They are learned rather in the same manner as language items are learned — empirically, by using them and noting how others use them.

The range of such systems extends far beyond taboos and reticence. There are, for instance, matters of privilege in speaking. In certain circumstances the 'right' to speak is accorded to certain individuals — for example, in lectures, or in sermons and speeches, while listeners are expected either to be silent or to express agreement or disagreement in certain ways — such as the parliamentary 'Hear! Hear!' Such privileges often go with one's profession. Schoolteachers insist on the right to speak and to be listened to in class and afford a similar privilege to pupils only on terms that they themselves try to define.

Social conventions do not affect merely the right to speak and the choice of subject matter. They go very deeply into the systems of categories and relationships that are themselves embodied in language. Category systems — classificatory devices — are necessary to efficient cognitive functioning. The 'case' for them is well understood. They are ways of economically managing vast ranges of data. They facilitate such processes as inferring and predicting without which immense extra labour would be necessary to cope with both everyday living and scholarly concerns. Such classificatory systems do not necessarily have linguistic correlates but in practice almost all of the most useful do. What we have as part of our inheritance, then, is a fairly comprehensive classificatory system which is embodied mainly in the lexis of language. Much of the classificatory work, but not all, is done by substantives — nouns and adjectives. For example, if we take the word 'desk', certain possibilities seem to come to mind. We begin to form a rough notion of what an object to which the word might properly refer might be like. Of course, our expectations may develop with time and experience. We may come to think that all desks have flat tops and that therefore any particular desk to which reference is made must have such a top. Our experience might then extend to a rolltop desk and so what might be classified in our mind as 'desk' is extended. Later still, we might find an example that is further from our initial image. Perhaps it is of a piece of flat wood which someone uses as a desk. We may not then be quite clear about whether this object is really a desk or whether there is not some implied comparison at work. In other words, the category system, which we use to anticipate and to predict as well as to create order, has rather vague and elastic boundaries. The same is true when we see a child playing at school. He might use anything as a desk — perhaps an ordinary table. Here we are in a world of pretence closely linked to that of metaphor. But the point to note is that however a category might change, however flexible it turns out to be, and however fuzzy it might be around the edges, it still has some noteworthy characteristics. These are that it is basically conventional and that it is a means of making effort economically. When we have allocated something to the category of desk we do expect it to have a flat top and to be suitable for writing on. We also may have less firm possibilities in mind. It may have legs and drawers. It may have a rolltop above its flat surface. It may be something else serving as a desk because of necessity or the requirements of play. The point is that we need little investigation to pin down these possibilities. We do not have to go back to the clean sheet and open mind situation and figure the whole thing out from the beginning. Moreover,

145

we also expect that members of the same speech community will have similar expectations and so we can use the classification in communicating as well as in thinking.

Such classifications are not restricted to nouns. If we say that something is 'yellow', we have a range of possibilities in mind. These, too, may be fuzzy around the edges (perhaps some colours are marginally better called 'green' than 'yellow', for example). But adjectives are in their way also classificatory devices. So, too, are verbs. 'To walk' is to engage in one of a number of similar but not identical ways of propelling oneself. Quite possibly no two people walk exactly the same, but classificatory devices, including verbs, are ways of treating phenomena that are separate and different as being somehow essentially the same. And to do this is itself a conventional way of proceeding, intimately bound up, as I have indicated, with language.

Just as language exemplifies and facilitates ways of classifying phenomena of very diverse kinds and thus enhances the processing power of cognition, so it also contains within itself ways of relating classes of phenomena to other classes, with the effect of further enhancing cognitive competence. Some of these ways are linked to the classificatory systems which have already been noted. Thus 'oaks' are a subclass of 'tree' and 'tree' is a supercategory of 'oak', 'elm', 'lime' and so on. Similarly, subordinate categories such as 'desk', 'table', 'chair' and so on relate to a superordinate category 'furniture'. Superordination and subordination immensely increase the convenience and power of the systems. So, too, does another flexibility allowed within our category systems. 'Oak' may belong with 'tree' or it may be part of an adjacent system which classifies it in relation to other deciduous trees, or of one which puts it with different sorts of timbers, such as the hardwoods. Or it may go along with inedibles in contrast to edibles. Here again, the learner has to find out what possibilities are available and to choose the appropriate one for his purposes. But the idea of what is appropriate is subject to cultural, and that means social, constraints.

Other relating systems are contained within the grammar. Time sequencing, possession, purpose, cause and effect and other relations are all expressible by means of grammatical systems. Following Whorf, we can say that such resources, which we note are conventional in their nature and are acquired more or less unconsciously, form a mould or template that is available for thought and communication.

As well as these resources for categorising and relating, language provides means for another sort of understanding and communication — that of discourse form. Although scholars have long been aware of and have argued about the potency of lexical and grammatical resources for thinking, it is only in recent years that attention has turned back to discourse and to the idea that it might be important as a mode of thinking and understanding as well as of communicating. In an earlier chapter I made a comparison with the notion of 'key' in music. Discourses — often they are longer, more or less complete stretches of language — hang together in certain ways and have an overall meaning potential which again is conventional and sometimes very subtle. At one extreme, we may compare discourse with metaphor, although it is difficult to accept any facile distinction between 'literal' and 'metaphorical' language. We can certainly say that in understanding how discourse works we get far away from the 'dictionary' view of language.

In order to illustrate this point, it may be useful to get away from language altogether and to take an instance that lies partly outside the realm of human behaviour. The principal actors are myself and my late dog, Chommy. Chommy was a golden Labrador, silly at times, a sedate gentleman at others, and completely unmalicious. Normally the most docile of creatures, he could nevertheless turn himself into a snarling, biting, teeth-baring, growling and seemingly ferocious beast. The point of my story is that he really did not mean it. Or rather, he meant it as play. When he received a sharp shove on the shoulder and saw a couple of hands sparring in front of him he would oblige by 'fighting'. His 'biting' consisted of nothing more than squeezing very firmly so as to leave red teeth marks, but never breaking the skin. He could, to please one, engage in play and in simulation. He seemed to enjoy it even when he was upended and pinned down, but he was wise as well as silly and it may be that he was only simulating enjoyment. It is clear that he understood that whole sequences of behaviour can have a significance different from that usually attributed to them. Once he understood the key, that it was to be a simulated fight, he was quite able to proceed and to further the enterprise. Play is perhaps a good example of a major discourse variety which itself contains subvarieties. But it is only a particularly vivid example of what is normal within language. In behaviour generally and within language activities, there is a 'key' to find, a 'wavelength' to which to tune and unless this is done the behaviour or language seems to be incomprehensible. It is this 'key' or 'wavelength' that determines how the signals shall be processed in order to make sense.

This understanding has to be learned. There is a parallel in Michael Halliday's famous address to the Nursery Schools Association. In his talk which was called 'Relevant Models of Language Use', Halliday identified some basic models of language use which he thought it was necessary for the child to understand if ever he was to comprehend and to use language for various and different purposes. These included the informational, the heuristic the imaginative and several others. Each model used language for a different purpose and tended to use it in distinctive ways to achieve that purpose. The idea of discourse-understanding extends this into the use of longer stretches of language. Thus there are distinctive ways of using language for different academic subjects and disciplines, and of using it ironically, of using it in journalistic writing and so on. They are somewhat akin to genres in the sense that the physical or aesthetic form which is the chief characteristic of each genre type may contain within itself discourse which may be of various kinds, some of which may be particularly associated with a particular genre. However, the characteristic which gives discourse its strength also makes it difficult to define; it is its flexibility. It may sometimes be marked (as play was with Chommy) by some non-linguistic behaviour. Sometimes the markers may be obvious signposts which stick out a mile. At other times they may be subtle and ambiguous in ways which set even highly experienced language users wondering. However, of one thing we can be sure. They are learned as most language is learned — not so much through direct instruction as through experience and experiment — through use, in fact.

In summary, we can say that language both lodges in the individual's memory and yet belongs in society. The locale in which it is learned is that of interpersonal relationships. Its intrapersonal use is founded upon language learned interpersonally. Man is moulded by language, not just by the transmission of its content, important as that often is. More importantly still, he is shaped constitutively by language in its cultural context, that is by language in use. Much of what we learn, we learn because it is locked into language. We have stressed the conventional nature of language, of its words and grammar of its systems of relationships, of its discourse styles, but of course a degree of inventiveness is always possible. Children playing with language often break into unconventional uses. And language extends its scope as its users coin neologisms, make striking metaphors, and deliberately use language unconventionally as James Joyce did. The constraints that language imposes can be broken — but only within limits. Such innovations are possible because of the conventional; they come into being by transcending it and their power comes because of their relation to it.

Language and cognitive processes

As language is acquired, it is used in certain cognitive processes. In most of these it has no exclusive role. But when it plays a part it often extends and strengthens what would otherwise be poorer without it. Both society and the life of the individual are characteristically (though by no means exclusively) linguistic — which is another way of saying that humans use language even when it might be possible to do without it. In what follows I shall select some functions which seem to me to be important and then I shall indicate what role language may typically play in those functions.

The first illustrates very well the point that even when language plays an optional role it may nevertheless be a significant one. Paying attention is among the most basic of the processes that I should call cognitive. It is often preliminary to, and also part of, other cognitive acts with which we shall deal later. Now, there is no doubt that prelinguistic children can pay attention. It is hardly an exaggeration to say that they do it for most of their waking hours. So, too, can non-linguistic animals. But in humans language enhances the process powerfully in three respects. In the first place, one can direct attention through language. Speaking to someone is an action which directs their attention. When words are uttered, labels enunciated, actions requested or demanded, questions asked, prompts given, these are all ways of directing attention. Thus, it is possible through linguistic negotiation to agree with someone else to look at or otherwise to sense or to consider something jointly. When language is used intrapersonally, the effect is the same. One can direct one's own attention by linguistic means. The older ones among us have been known to mutter the name of whatever we seek as we wander into another room in search of something. There is no sharp division between these two examples of directing attention and the third of the functions which one ascribes to language, which is that of sustaining that attention, of keeping it focused when once it has been directed.

I dealt above with classifying and relating. The attention-directing and attention-sustaining roles of language tend to overlap with those of classifying and relating. All are important in a third cognitive area — that of memorising and recall.

In the section on reading I introduced briefly the idea of short-term memory, pointing out that its limited capacity and its essentially temporary nature made it difficult to read slowly because as slow readers decoded to sound they might lose the gist of what they had previously processed for meaning.

Although it is useful to speak of 'limited capacity' in this way, it is important to understand that the metaphor which allows us to speak of memory as though it were a sort of filing system can be seriously misleading, for memory is much more than that. If, for example, we successfully read a story what is it that we shall remember of it? As we are reading it, we might remember verbatim what we have immediately read. The same, incidentally, would apply to memories of a conversation. For a short time we might remember word for word what had just been said. But as with reading, this memory would soon fade and would be replaced by similar memories as one proceeded with whatever language was being encountered. What is remembered in the longer term is not word-for-word, however, but gist, something closer to the essence and this is done without any necessary conscious effort to refine or memorise it. And so we can say that memory is an inherently dynamic process. Moreover, this process tends to be recurrent or continuous, for our accounts of gist will change with time. As we attempt later recall, what normally happens is that we move further away from the verbatim and also further away from detail and towards a more concentrated version of the gist. If challenged, I should admit at once that it is possible for the individual to some extent to override, or at least counteract this process. One can keep closer to the verbatim or closer to the mass of detail but only to a limited extent, and only by conscious effort.

Walter Kintsch makes a useful distinction between different sorts of memory — one which adds to our understanding of the processes involved. In his essay 'Episodic and Semantic Memory' he draws a distinction between these two sorts of memory. *Episodic memory*, he says, receives and stores — temporally and spatially — marked information about events or episodes. He uses 'events and episodes', of course, to mean psychological events and episodes. They may be important or they may be trivial. They may or may not have any bearing on any longer story. Whether what is stored is trivial or not, it is always autobiographical. Moreover, the 'when' and the 'how' of the happening are just as important as the 'what'.

Semantic memory, on the other hand, is an organised store of knowledge about the world (and about language and its use). It has transcended or 'processed out' the particularities of time and place and manner. It is based on personal experiences, but they are transformed through such processes as abstraction and generalisation into items of knowledge and are then integrated with other knowledge. A fascinating characteristic of this sort of knowledge, incidentally, is that it permits the retrieval of information that was never stored in the first place, at least not directly through sensory mechanisms, for in part it is the product of inferences.

Kintsch goes on to make two points about semantic memory that are especially valuable from our point of view. Encoding into memory is a vital part of the process. Kintsch suggests that this is done as remembered items are seen in terms of certain features which are then, somehow, encoded. It is the depth and richness of this encoding that is a primary determinant of how well something will be remembered. What he calls 'organisation', by which he means the elaboration of relationships among the items is an especially important form of encoding. His second point is that both encoding and retrieval depend heavily on context, with retrieval depending upon reinstating the context of the encoding.

Kintsch, it seems to me, does justice to the idea of memory as a dynamic processing house and takes us well beyond the notion of memory as a file. Further, his idea that such processing includes inferencing stresses its kinship with other complex psychological activities, such as reading and listening for meaning. Also, it accounts in psychological terms for the distinction between learning — any learning — and acquiring knowledge.

What seems remarkable to me is the role that language might play in these processes. Semantic memory, in particular, seems to be redolent of language. The encodings, the contexts within which encoding takes place, the abstracting and generalising, the organisation or relating what is learned to other items may all have linguistic correlates and work through linguistic means. While it would be going too far to claim that language has an exclusive role to play, it would be safe to make the more modest claim that its role is likely to be powerful and often indispensable. And if we allow that, we are saying that a very great deal of our knowledge, stored in the memory of the individual is language-based or language-related.

Teachers' Language

The language used by the teacher is always important, her speech even more so than her writing. In the first place, it is a model for children of how language can be used. All of us need to come to a sort of deep learning about the uses to which language can be put — this was Halliday's theme in 'Relevant Models of Language' and I have extended the idea to include discourse. The child does not just learn language items; he learns that language can be used for certain purposes and in certain ways and he learns this, for the most part, from models around him. Now, no matter how linguistically rich the home is, it is the case that certain sorts of language are more likely to be employed in the school than in the home. In school, that is, language items are going to be selected, combined and used in different ways. The teacher is the young child's principal adult model outside the family. Her aim should therefore be to use her own language resources widely. Often it does not matter if the children do not fully comprehend as long as they remain engaged in whatever is going on. When they are engaged, the teacher has no need to be afraid of using new vocabulary, or of employing unusual grammatical constructions and variations in her style — as long as they are examples of legitimate and appropriate uses of language in the circumstances. There is a zone of familiarisation into which all who are learning to use language must enter. Fully secure learning and confident use come later.

It may also be that the teacher is the bridge from whatever linguistic mores prevail in the family to the principles that govern the polite, tactful, and suitably reticent uses of language in the wider community. Because language enshrines so much in the way of attitudes, there are dangers here, as well as opportunities. Nothing is more personal or sensitive than one's own use of language, especially when it seems to be under scrutiny by others. There is, therefore, an absolute need for the teacher to act always with tact and with respect towards her children. Her aim, after all, is to increase the competence of her children, and the way ahead is by adding to their linguistic resources and not by subtracting from them.

The teacher must also provide a model for conversation. Opening and closing conversations and conducting the give-and-take and the turntaking are never easy and have to be learned. The implications of this insight are far-reaching. In the first place, they seem to indicate what sort of a teacher she should be — close enough to children to engage with them in such conversations. They also determine what she should seek to do with much of her time — and that is to seek out opportunities of talking with each child. The suggestions we have made for conferences or chats about books and about reading and writing may be useful here. Lunchtimes and playtimes, periods before and after school, visits, also give her her chances. Time spent in 'real' conversation may help the child towards the most fruitful learning of his day.

There is one other sense in which the teacher should provide a model — that is in clearly articulating what she says. This, of course, does not mean that she should talk in a stilted or artificial way. Nor should she give what might be thought of in a mechanical way as 'full value' to every sound. She should use language as it is used in life, with all the elisions, slurs, and individual variations that are normal in informal language. On the other hand, she should speak with more deliberate articulation when she comes to use more formal language. Children need to learn that it is legitimate to use either — when the circumstances are right — and they need the practice in coping with both.

This brings us to a negative principle founded on a positive principle. The negative principle is that the teacher should avoid managerial language as far as possible. Managerial language is the language used to control noise level and behaviour generally, to marshall children and to remonstrate with them. Of course, some use of this sort of language is necessary. But children learn little from it except to pay little attention to its finer points (if indeed, there are any). The danger to the teacher is that she can feel to be very busy using language for most of the day to children and yet it could be this sort which is counterproductive. Of course, some language of this sort is unavoidable but it should be kept to a minimum. The positive principle is that, as I hinted above, the psychological distance between teacher and taught should be as close as practicalities permit. The teacher is not one of the gang, nor is she the mother and she cannot be in a similar relation to the child as is any of these. Nevertheless, if language is to flow productively, she needs to be fairly close and this is why managerial language, with its distancing effects, has its dangers, especially if it becomes dominant.

I said above that the teacher's spoken language was more important than her writing and, while this is true, it does not mean that her writing is not also important. I have already mentioned some of the ways in which it is. The teacher provides product and process models for handwriting. She can help the child by acting as a scribe to convert his spoken composition into writing. She may collaborate with a child in joint authorship, She may be an author in her own right, demonstrating something of the process of wrestling with her texts in order to make the reader's job easier. Her task is basically to be a living reminder that all texts have authors and to educate the children into more sophisticated understandings of what it is to be a writer.

Similar considerations apply to her reading. She should read and be able to talk in detail about many of the books that her children are reading, and she should discuss with them the problems that they encounter in the business of getting meaning from the texts.

Finally, we come to language in the communal life of the school. School assembly gives the opportunities for the most diverse array of language of all. There is the language the Head may use to welcome, to inform and to admonish — language from which the children will learn deeply — for example, about what sort of place the school really is and what sort of people are in charge of them. There is the language of prayer — even more diverse in a multicultural society than it was in the past. There is the language of various dramatic and musical presentations that children may offer to the school community. There is the language of outsiders who may come in to speak to the school. The best assemblies are nothing less than aesthetic and linguistic treasuries, full of splendours.

Section 2: study skills

One of the major themes, stressed throughout this book, has been that learning to make meanings necessarily involves learning a great deal about the world, the people in it and how they behave. It involves being inducted into a particular culture and learning a great deal about this culture implicitly through language.

Now we turn to confront the more deliberate use of language for learning at the point where it becomes the instrument and tool of learning rather than being only a necessary concomitant to it. We are in the worlds of education and schooling.

Study skills are important in education. Indeed, to a large extent education is about fostering them and about using them in learning. Yet it seems to me that not enough attention is paid by teachers at all levels to their development with the result that, even in

higher education, students in colleges and universities are handicapped because their skills are not adequate to meet the demands
that are made upon them. Nevertheless it is unusual, in this country
at least, for the formal pursuit of such skills to be a significant part
of the students' learning agenda, possibly because it is assumed that
the skills ought to have been mastered earlier in a child's career.
There is something in this, but it is only a half-truth. No doubt,
much of this learning should have been effected earlier, but there
is always much to learn both about the business of studying and
in perfecting its operational skills. This is partly because an element
of subject specificity is always involved and, although much of what
is learned in one area can be applied elsewhere, this is only the case
to a certain degree. In other words, study skills are not completely
monolithic — they differ according to what is being learned. Nor
is subject matter the only variable in the process, for it is also affected
by perceptions about the reasons and purposes that lie behind the
learning. Also, the scope and quality of the learning are affected
by the extent of the learner's prior knowledge and by its status in
his mind. This may seem obvious to us but the point is that, as
the learner becomes more sophisticated, he needs to be conscious
of these matters and to use them to govern his learning behaviour.

Much has been written about study skills in recent years. Some
of it, at least, has been misguided. There is no need to publish books
which purport to 'teach' such skills to children and students. In
essence, study skills are the same as those we have been talking about
throughout this book, with some extensions. It is because they are
affected by so many variables and also because some of these
variables are personal to the learner that the publication of books
of exercises is likely to be wrong in principle. Moreover, as I shall
argue later, 'exercises' tend to ignore the needs of communication
which provide us with one of the keys to the pupil's success.

Study skills are essentially a development of what has been
learned from the first moments of language and even earlier. In
Halliday's famous paper to the Nursery Schools Association he
outlined various models of language use which the young child
needed to discern before he could go on to use language for similar
purposes. One of these was the heuristic model in which language
is used for the purpose of finding out. In a nutshell, the development
of study skills is the extension and elaboration of this sort of language
use into modes of investigative behaviour, and it is here that there
lies the continuity between what is learned in the home in the early
months of life and what is learned and applied in school, in

155

university and in later life. Our task is now to examine this development and to identify those elements that will enable teachers to understand their own roles as they, in turn, help their children.

Comprehension, it seems to me, is the heart of study skills. Because of this, reading and listening, which involve comprehension, are the language skills with which we shall be mainly concerned, but the other language skills also play a part. Earlier, we referred to certain 'extensions' which take us beyond the sort of skills learned earlier. Perhaps the most important of these is that the child now has to learn to identify and often how to locate what has to be comprehended. This is the basis of the so-called 'library skills' that are rightly taken to be an important part of study skills. There is no harm in thinking of these as 'library skills' as long as it is understood that we are now dealing with deep structures of knowledge and that referencing and indexing skills and such like are only the tip of a very large iceberg.

Skills for finding out what?

A major fault with typical treatments of study skills, one that is enshrined in many books of exercises, is the tendency to treat the finding out of information as their main purpose. It would be much more helpful to make it clear that this could only begin to be acceptable as long as 'information' meant something more than facts. Of course, one possible object of using study skills is to collect facts, but study includes much more than this. It involves the students in discerning relationships of various kinds, in forming concepts and principles, in achieving understandings and so on. It necessitates the alteration, by extension or by deepening, of knowledge structures that already exist in the learner.

Once we grasp that we are not restricted to the acquisition of facts, we have to agree to open up the whole range of study skills. We need no longer concentrate on the transmission of facts and can deal with other matters as diverse, for example, as strategies for judging the truth or falsity or relevance of propositions and with the processes of negotiation seen as a means of achieving understandings. Study skills are not mainly mechanical; they are more than finding out — more, even, than negotiating. They involve changing the very constitution of the learner.

Two sets of work by distinguished contributors are worth noting in this respect. The first, the Humanities Curriculum Project with which the late Professor L. Stenhouse was associated, was a way of getting youngsters — usually adolescents — to examine salient issues such as matters of the relationship between the sexes, war and peace, poverty, and so on. The issues were presented in a variety of ways — through fiction and poetry or by way of articles or extracts from academic books. Much of the skill of the teacher lay in the selection and presentation of suitable material to whatever group she was working with. The members of the group then discussed the issues. The teacher's role at this stage was that of neutral chairman whose function did not extend either to passing or to outlining opinions herself. The issues were, of course, essentially moral questions. Empirical facts impinged, as they always do, but the basic matters were linked to 'ought' rather than to 'are'. In other words, the enterprise was neither an investigation into, nor a collection of, facts. It was intended to work at different levels.

When the scheme went well, there was often silence in the group and this might be followed by tentative statements and by arguments which relied on personal experiences, by declarations of the principles they seemed to support and by other arguments which appealed to more abstract reasons. There were two outcomes that should interest us. The first was the way in which children took different points of view into account. The second, which depended on the first, was the difference between the positions at which various individuals started and those at which they finished. Both outcomes show the results of study skills — skills used to gain knowledge — in action.

The second contributor whose work we also need briefly to consider is Douglas Barnes. As part of his immensely valuable work on the role of language in learning, he presented children in small groups with a well-chosen poem and got them to accept the task of discussing it. The poem was intended to be somewhat on the outer edges of the children's understanding. What followed was often fascinating and happened in the absence of the teacher. Children would consider bits of text in the light of other bits of text or of their own experiences. Sometimes they might move off into seeming irrelevancies. But, even if they did so, they would return to the text, usually illuminating it further. The point, of course, is that at the end of the process there had usually been an enhancement of understanding, not, it should be noted, as it might have been if a lecturer had explicated the text to them, but an extension that might be significantly different from child to child. It was not a matter of arriving at approved answers, so much as of being involved in a process which led, through understanding, to a deeper kind of mental growth.

The wider view of the scope of study skills, and in particular the inclusion of what Barnes calls 'negotiation', takes us well beyond simple comprehension and much further than traditional library skills. We must also include skills in discussing, which are based partly upon comprehension, partly upon the ability to participate in discourse of a certain kind. As well as the skills of engaging in conversations, such as turntaking, we must include the use of language to convey propositions, to make arguments, to persuade others, and so on.

This bring us to an important principle that is often ignored by text books which 'teach' study skills. It is that the communication of what is found out, or the communication of one's own opinions, in as realistic a setting as possible — one, that is, in which the participant feels that it is important to communicate — can become a major part of the process. Not all study is for the purpose of engaging with others, but much of it is. Real communication pushes one into being clear about what one knows or thinks and exercises the ability to discern the needs of the listener, as far as they are defined by the limits of his existing knowledge. The need to communicate is therefore both highly motivating and formative. If it is to be completely successful it demands insights into other people's minds and eventually into knowledge itself. Often these insights will depend quite as much on hunches and intuitions as on discerned facts. Study which is to result in a talk, a discussion, a book, or a set of private notes may involve different processes of understanding, each being shaped by the purpose for which it is intended. And study which is intended to bring to one a bare outline of a subject area will be different from study which is intended to amass great detail about the same area.

Thus, there are different sorts of outcomes and different sorts of intensities and part of the skill of the successful student is to be able to operate in different ways as different principles govern the operation. This demands maturity and a certain detachment which are alredy coming into view in the primary years. To refer in this way to detachment is to take us into the realms of attitudes and it is this territory that we next explore.

Attitudes

It may well be that certain attitudes are both the crucial hallmark and the necessary condition of successful development. In connection with the formation of such attitudes I should like to consider, again very briefly, examples from two American and one British source.

The first of these is the work of Marion Blank which she related in her book *Teaching Learning in the Pre-School: a Dialogue Approach*.

Blank was mainly concerned with the poor performance of young children in such matters as the discrimination of sounds, categorisation, the analysis of complex visual patterns, the recall of stories and perceptual-motor discrimination. She was impressed by the overall and global nature of her children's failure and concluded, therefore, that something more radical was needed than the mere teaching of skills. She shifted her focus away from the child's attainments and tried to develop an inclination, or attitude, which would characterise the whole of an individual's response to his environment. Other workers have sought a roughly similar end, though they called it by different names, as Blank noted. Deutsch, for example, called it merely 'attention', Werner 'conceptual representation' (in contrast with 'perceptual representation'). Witkin called it 'field-independence' and Goldstein 'the abstract attitude'. Blank adopted Goldstein's term and also that writer's stress on such factors as the child's ability to shift reflectively from one aspect of a situation to another and voluntarily to evoke experiences to keep in mind various different aspects of a task. Blank noted the resistance and anxiety that increasingly became associated with failure in the school setting. She stressed that 'the overriding quality of the content of the abstract attitude is sustained sequential thinking', and set about fostering it. She also stressed the importance of context to a particular task and the need for the child to take that into account. In this she can be compared to others such as Margaret Donaldson and her colleagues, and Valerie Walkerdine who have also seen context and the child's perception of that context as being crucial. For Blank, context became increasingly important as chains of events extending into time and space had to be understood.

> To be able to see objects, events and words as located within their appropriate framework, the child must be able to maintain concentration and evaluate the information that is available to him. The opportunity for the sustained pursuit

of an idea if of vital importance is critical to the way in which the abstract attitude is acquired.

As far as her approaches to fostering are concerned, Blank was deeply suspicious of group activity: it did not necessarily demand sustained attention from an individual; it was dilute, sporadic and it allowed children 'to hide' or 'to rest'; and perhaps worst of all, it allowed failure to go undiagnosed. In its place she proposed a dialogue approach which would make demands that would require the child to analyse his perceptual field and where the verbal element would serve him as an organising guide. She felt that major advances would come when the question-form became internalised — when the child began to ask questions of himself as part of a search for hypotheses. 'Once everything can be questioned, the child is no longer restrained by reality, he is only restrained by the limits of his imagination in inventing alternatives to what exists.'

She linked this to Jerome Bruner's idea of symbolic representation which gave the child the means 'for experimental alteration of the environment without having, so to speak, to raise a finger by way of trial and error or to picture anything in the mind's eye by imagery'.

'Symbolic representation' was Bruner's third mode of representing the world in the mind. It came into use after the enactive and the iconic modes which were based on action and image respectively. It did not replace them and they went on being used. But it certainly reduced their relative importance. The symbols in question were mainly linguistic and their use in this way, as Bruner points out, greatly amplified what the mind was capable of doing — both extending what it could take into account and increasing the complexity of what it could do with it.

To some in Britain, Blank's work seemed to involve teachers in hooking children very firmly and then refusing to let them off the hook, so that it was even thought to amount to harshness. This is not the time to discuss such objections, however. From the present point of view the importance of Blank's work is the importance she attached to underlying attitude, for it was attitudes which governed the way in which skills operated and therefore the ways in which they developed. It is also worth noting the great value she placed upon language both in conversation and in its 'internal' use by the child to focus, to switch attention to various aspects of whatever was being regarded and to reflect upon alternatives.

My second example is also American. It is from the work of

James Moffett, as outlined in his book, *Teaching the Universe of Discourse*, a seminal work. From our present point of view, the book contains two significant features. The first is his stress on the importance of discourse as a way both of understanding and of operating. The second, which is closer to Blank's ideas, is his belief that if certain language forms and their functions could be first internalised and then become self-initiated in use, significant mental growth would occur. He said 'I would like to advance a hypothesis that dialogue is the major means of developing thought and language.' He considered that two general limitations characterised the speech and thought of both younger and older, but disadvantaged, children. The first was a failure to specify. The second was a failure to relate. The first he saw as an act of analysis, the second as one of synthesis. The verbally immature needed both to discriminate and to specify more — to move towards details and also to connect, especially in casual, temporal, and contrastive ways and to subordinate ideas one to another. Thus the growth needed to be in two opposite directions — towards greater detail and specificity and towards greater abstraction. Moffett singled out certain dialogue operations that he thought would help to teach the elaboration of speech and thought. Among these operations were asking questions and giving answers, and getting children to append qualifying clauses as, for example, when an 'if' is introduced as in 'He'll make it if he finds the key.' 'The true *because*,' he said, 'is born of *why?*'

Thus Moffett, too, was concerned with underlying trends of development — with what was essential if skills were to be further developed and used successfully. He, just as much as Blank, tried to build up a set or attitude — a way of handling communicating and thinking that would be a foundation for much that a person might later wish to attempt.

The third example is drawn from the work of Eric Lunzer and Keith Gardner at the University of Nottingham. Their work was on 'The Effective Use of Reading'; their concern was with using reading to learn. They were dismissive of any simple approach through skills. Like Blank, they searched for something which was deeper than skills but which would govern the way in which reading behaviour was controlled by the reader. The contribution that they and their team made, not only in the 'Effective Use of Reading' programme but also later when they turned more specifically to 'Reading To Learn' is notable in many respects. It is rather a sad commentary on the parochialism of our profession that it has

161

tended to be ignored by many primary teachers simply because it was directed at older children. It is certain that their work as a whole says many important things about reading, its characteristics, the ways in which it can be learned, the nature of comprehension, the development of study skills and much more. For these reasons, their books ought to be required reading for all teachers.

Important as their conclusions are, they are not uncontroversial. Their denial that reading comprehension could be broken down into a series of subskills is true from one point of view and, I think, misleading from another. It is salutary in that it rejects the old-fashioned and crude notion that there is a hierarchy of skills, perhaps beginning with decoding to sound and ending maybe with library skills that must be learned in sequence, with comprehension really only figuring in the later stages. Lunzer and Gardner were wise, too, in believing that there was something else beyond, or beneath skills. But those who remember the early pages of this present book will, I hope, understand that it is not necessary to dispose of both baby and bathwater. It is perfectly possible to adhere to the notion of skills and to build these into a more complete picture of what reading really is. Moreover, when we turn to learning to read, the skills approach provides us with a bonus. It offers useful models of how reading might be learned — with an emphasis on practice, on feedback, on real reading and on fostering in the reader an understanding of what reading is. In this way he can reach an increasingly sophisticated view of what it is that he is trying to learn and he can then begin to shape his learning accordingly.

However, to argue such matters is not the main purpose of this present chapter which is to consider Lunzer's and Gardner's insistence on what is a necessary prerequisite to true comprehension. From the evidence they gathered, they concluded that 'individual differences in reading comprehension should be thought of as the ability to reflect on what is being read'. They recognised that this ability was neither simple nor innate but felt that it could be enhanced by appropriate reading strategies. Their further conclusion 'that a prime consideration should be the involvement of pupils in their reading' is impeccable. They believe that teachers of English are constantly engaged in the effort to find texts which will excite their pupils' imaginations, and that this is itself a probable prerequisite of reflection. They see grave problems in subject areas, however, asking 'How does one create a willingness to reflect on a physics text or on an historical treatise?' They are also clear that even when the pupil is willing to reflect, there is a further problem concerning the quality of that reflection which, they recognise, may be variable. They agree that this will depend on the quality of existing knowledge and also on methods of study which can refine 'the purposeful search of the printed text'. Their book is very much about fostering this 'purposeful search'.

And so, from the work of Blank, Moffett, Garden and Lunzer alike comes this insistence that attitude is basically important. All seem to agree, though they do not put it this way, that the process is cumulative, prior work (and I should myself insist, prior success) building good attitudes. Good attitudes both motivate the child and allow him to work at greater depth, in effect transforming the task in the process. Success builds better attitudes and so there is an ascending spiral. Here I cannot resist harking back to the earlier criticism that I levelled against the tendency rigidly to divide the linguistic from the emotional and both from the intellectual and so on. Attitudes, I suppose, may be regarded as being part of the orectic domain, along with emotions, impulses and so on. But I want to insist that they are formed through a process that might just as well be called intellectual (or cognitive) or linguistic and that their force is also felt in these areas as much as it is anywhere else.

Knowledge and study skills

Knowledge is both the aim of study skills and also their directing force. Investigation and enquiry are carried on in the diverse ways which I have outlined earlier. It is not possible to take a narrow view of the processes involved. Not one of them works in the dark. Now, it is true that sometimes we do not know what we are going to learn until we have learned it, and we may be surprised when it happens. But, more or less, the acquisition of knowledge is effected in rather the same way as a builder builds a house. Trial and error, especially of the blind 'charge the cage and see what happens' sort which desperate animals might possibly adopt, is quite rare. We have stressed throughout the importance of expectations, and once again they become significant. Much knowledge is acquired because one anticipates both the process and the outcome. This is not to say that all knowledge is to be acquired with perfect clarity, only that anticipations based upon one's present knowledge enter into the process to a greater or lesser degree. Moreover, this process can become increasingly self-conscious and reflexive. Anticipations, expectations, the use of prior knowledge help to set our strategies. One makes a map of subjects and their interrelationships and one uses the map as one advances into new territory. There is thus a continuum from the less to the more self-conscious and reflexive. It is not unusual that the great explorers and many of the great scientific discoverers have actually been looking for what they eventually found. Stumbling across something by accident does, of course, happen, but time and time again such discoveries await reappraisal, sometimes by later generations in the light of their other knowledge.

At this point it would be as well to indicate what I mean by knowledge. It is not the same as learning, though learning is always involved in the acquisition of knowledge. Such knowledge may be of facts or it may be of understandings. Even when it is of facts, it is never 'raw'. Sensory data, for example, do not in themselves constitute knowledge. When light waves impinge on the nerves of the eye, that is not knowledge: when sounds are picked up through the ear, that is not knowledge. Knowledge can only come when other psychological processes have been at work. When there is generalisation, or abstraction, or the relating of sensory events to existing knowledge structures, then there is knowledge. Such knowledge can be formed largely in an empirical sphere, dealing with sensory input in the ways I have suggested. Or, it can be more reflective, dealing in a more remote way with sensory data that have already been processed. It can also come about through making inferences and deductions, by as it were, leaping ahead.

A little earlier, I used the term 'discovery' in connection with new knowledge, but this is only partly correct. It would perhaps be more apt to refer to the 'formulation' of knowledge.

Knowledge is not necessarily true, but it is invariably (though perhaps tentatively) believed to be true. A hypothesis has, I believe, status as knowledge. But, by definition, it is put forward in a tentative way, as a means of furthering knowledge. This brings us to an important point. Some knowledge is substantive — final at least for the time being. Other knowledge, of which the hypothesis is an example, is procedural. Study skills, I have said, involve the use of prior knowledge. Now I should add that some of this knowledge is procedural, concerned with truth mechanisms of different kinds. Such mechanisms do in fact differ according to the area in which one operates. Truth mechanisms — procedures for finding and validating the truth — differ greatly among themselves. Those concerned with, say, the natural sciences are different from those concerned with, for example, theology or philosophy. Because of this, study skills must also differ in these areas. This is why we earlier emphasised that important places among them must be found for 'negotiation' and the willingness to reflect.

Education is, I believe, very much a process of equipping learners to manage such matters. It is about building knowledge and it is about building the equipment that will help the learner to acquire and evaluate such knowledge for himself. What the learner needs is a map, a series of models and a set of procedures that will allow him to evaluate the status both of his own claims to knowledge and those of others.

The map that children need is a mental map that shows subjects and disciplines, what their distinctive concerns are, and how they relate to one another. The map is drawn as learning takes place and, like much other learning, this learning can go on at different levels. At one level the task is formidable enough to engage the attention of great philosophers and to provoke them to disagreements among themselves. At a lower level, it involves children in getting a rough idea of what a subject is supposed to be about. Later, it entails coming to know what methods a subject or discipline employs. This, too, is done at different levels. At one end are the formulations of, say, Karl Popper, about the methods of science; at the other end are the observations of plants made by very young children who learn as they make them that observation is an important method of science. This knowledge is cumulative, and it is perhaps a reflection on teacher training procedures in this country that the study of how it develops is not given greater prominence in the training departments of polytechnics and universities. Certainly, the more that teachers know about it, the more they will be able to help youngsters.

The map thus leads to the models which are mental formulations about the ways of proceeding employed by various subjects and disciplines. The models show both the distinctive concerns of each domain on the map and its ways of pursuing those concerns. Development is, I suspect, along two dimensions. The first is of increasing understanding and awareness of subjects and their methods. The second is a dimension which is probably more reflexive and self-conscious. It is the one concerned with appropriateness. Along it we shall find increasingly sophisticated answers to such questions as: what is the appropriate method here? What are we trying to find out? Shall we end with fact or opinion? Are we in a hypothetical and empirical or reflective and rational mode?

What will be the status of our results? Thus we are in the same world of epistemology as we were in when we travelled the first dimension. In terms of personal development we contemplate a growth in reflexivity — a state of knowing, of knowing that we know and knowing the status of that knowledge. So we can say that the direction in which the teacher wants the child to go lies well beyond the 'results' of any particular investigation whether that is empirical, or aesthetic or normative. It lies in the mind of the student — in the growth of reflexivity, of the child's idea of himself as a learner and knower, of the sorts of understandings that he possesses, of the status that these understandings possess — whether they are factual, opinion, hypothetical, judgements of moral value, guesses. The point is that these are the real, though sometimes the incidental, aims of study skills. And they are not merely reflexive, they are practical — for they influence what is done, how it should be tackled and, of course, the way we regard the outcomes.

Using the language skills as study skills

I have said a good deal about the role of speaking and listening among the study skills. When we take the extended view of study skills for which I have argued, that role is seen to be vital. There can, for instance, be no negotiated learning without speech. And if Blank and Moffett are right, both attitudes and procedures can be internalised through listening to spoken language and engaging in dialogue. One of the ways in which this might work is through the use of questions. The actual form of the question is important. There is a stage of development or perhaps a frame of mind in which children wish to tell what they know rather than answer questions about it. Some questions demand a 'yes' or 'no' answer. They have their uses in the early stages and later on in 'lubricating' dialogues. Later come questions of the 'wh' type — those that ask why?, when? and where? and their close cousin how? which cannot be answered by a 'yes' or 'no'. What becomes crucial is the ability to understand the question. What does 'why?' mean? What sort of answer does it require? This kind of understanding precedes the ability to use such questions internally and independently.

Mention of such understanding brings us again to discourse-understanding and back again to our old notion of 'key'. In order to be able to engage in discourse — whether to understand it or to produce it — one must have this key. And so we can say that among the most important of all study skills are those which enable the learner to find this key. Again this is not so much a matter of direct teaching, though it may be useful from time to time to bring the problems of finding the key explicitly to the notice of children. In the main, however, it is a matter of long-term and extensive learning with the teacher playing something of a background role as motivator and of occasional sharpener-up.

When children are asked to use work cards they often look upon the 'questions', whether or not they are in the interrogative form, as invitations to pursue a certain sort of action. In other words they feel themselves to be in a discursive situation and they seek the key. Such keys may be far away from the card itself, buried deep in the teacher's assumptions. If we move from work cards to examination questions, we can see the force of this even more clearly. 'What were the causes of the Great War?' does not mean that the candidate should list those causes in however brief a way as he may choose. It means also 'Spend about an hour in writing your answer. Do not dare merely to list those causes. Instead, argue for them and perhaps against alternative explanations. Explain the ways in which the causes operated and examine also the relative strength of each cause.' It is only when the student realises that these are cast-iron requirements that he is likely to do well in his examination. All teachers know that they expect children to perform tasks in ways that are often narrowly precise but unstated. The point is that when faced with questions, including oral questions and those in the 'task' sections of text books, children may need some help in understanding the particular discourse value of the question.

So when children are asked to study or to search, they need to know first of all what sort of enterprise they are being engaged in. Is it the pursuit of fact? Is it going to be the making of a value judgement, or the forming of an opinion? Then they need to know what sort of discourse they are being asked to follow. What sort of answer, of what length and of what detail will they need?

Then they may have, especially if they are seeking information, to make what I should call a 'broad search'. It is at this point that a knowledge of subjects and their organisation — of the map to which we referred earlier — is needed. Of course, the child's task can be made easier by telling him where on the knowledge map the information that he is seeking can be found. Whether or not he is left to his own devices, he then needs to know not just how knowledge is organised in the world generally, but specifically how it is organised in the sources to which he has access. Moving from one sort of organisation to another is often a source of major difficulty. And it is made more difficult by the absence of uniformity in libraries and books. For example, one library may be organised on a simple distinction between fiction and non-fiction. Another may use the Dewey system. Another may use an alternative which is just as detailed. One encylopaedia may be organised alphabetically and another, such as the Oxford Children's Encylopaedia, on lines which takes rather idiosyncratic clusters of subjects as the theme for each volume and then organises each volume on alphabetic lines. And so, what the child grows up with is, on the one hand, his own map of subjects and, on the other, a growing catalogue of alternative organisations of knowledge that he finds in libraries and books. In the long run what the child needs in order to cope is a knowledge of general subject areas and an understanding of their near neighbours and close relations. It is this sort of knowledge that gives the resourcefulness and the resilience that are needed for more mature investigation — it is knowing what to do when one comes up against a seeming dead-end.

The phase of what I call 'the narrow search' — that of finding information from sources that are to hand — is sometimes thought to be the major part of 'study skills'. It is true that the skills which are pertinent here — such as the 'library skills' — can be taught reasonably separately from the wider contexts that we have been discussing. It is certain that from to time they do require an intensive focus from both teacher and taught. But any separation should only be temporary. And it is a profound mistake to take the part for the whole. Simply to teach 'library skills' comes from a misunderstanding of what investigation is. It ignores the necessity to learn and to use knowledge of diverse sorts — only some of which are factual. It ignores, too, the need for a subject map, the possession of which in increasingly sophisticated form, I have argued, is the hallmark of the educated person. And, most sadly, it leaves high and dry the investigator who is faced with initial failure. And all of this comes of mistaking the tip for the iceberg.

Once the investigator has found a possible source in a book, he needs to mobilise various skills. He needs to look at the table of contents and, possibly, at the index. He needs to know, therefore, how these might be organised. Even this narrow search depends on his having an overview, on his knowing the sort of thing that he is looking for and on his knowing or suspecting something about adjacent and inclusive subjects. His eventual success will depend on what he knows and on the accessibility of what he is seeking.

But the task of finding out can be intrinsically difficult; those who spend time professionally seeking such information know that it is not easy at any level. Because of this, the child will need a good deal of encouragement and there is always a danger of overburdening him. When that happens he either begins to work at a low level, perhaps slavishly copying chunks of his sources that may have little relevance, or he becomes frustrated. The teacher needs to bear these possibilities in mind. She can help by looking to the ease with which sources are accessible and by making sure that the child understands exactly what he is supposed to be doing at any stage in the proceedings.

When a child has located a text, he must then employ strategies to deal with it. There are ways of surveying and skimming texts in order to extract certain minimal information and children need to be assured that there are times when it is right to use them. There are also ways of practising these strategies — preferably using real texts and, often, in the form of games.

It is now well-established that knowledge of what is called story grammar, but which I should prefer to call story structure, is also valuable to the child in three main ways. First, it provides him with a sort of tentative map or diagram by means of which to find his way around the text of a new story. He knows how, and within limits, when events are sequenced, settings laid, characters introduced, complications ensue and resolutions reached. Second, this same structure is a help in later recall. Third, it provides him with a structure for his own story writing. We return once more, let it be noted, to the interdependence of the skills. And, we should add, it is not just fictional story that has its distinctive structures. 'True' narrative also follows lines that closely resemble those of fiction. As we move further away from narrative, say into expository writing, the structure changes more noticeably. But there are still 'rules' for introducing topics and elaborating them, of summarising what has been written and moving on to new themes. Writers make assumptions about what information they must pass in their texts and these assumptions, once recognised by the reader, are a help to comprehension.

What I am insisting on is that the reader needs to build up and to use a knowledge of the architecture of whatever genre he is studying. He will do so through many encounters and over a long period of time. Occasionally, though, the teacher might help by analysing a well-chosen piece with a child with the idea of strengthening this sort of knowledge — it is really a more generalised sort of expectation that the child needs to bring to texts.

Methods of dealing with whole texts, of which the use of story structure is one, are, I believe, close to the heart of study skills. What the child seeks is gist — with enough detail to suit the purpose for which he is studying. Because this idea of purpose governs the amount of detail, it is essential that he should be clear about it. It is sometimes a tough problem and one that even undergraduates do not always solve. Possibly the important point for teachers to remember is that the child's weighing-up of purpose and the consequent regulating of his detail-getting behaviour are crucial. They are an essential part of study skills. And so they ought to be given due prominence. The teacher should show that she recognises their importance by explicitly discussing how one's estimate of purpose should affect what one then does. The temptation to get children too quickly into the 'busy' activities of searching for sources and reading texts needs to be resisted and due place given to the more thoughtful consideration of purpose and scope. Considering these is part of what it is to be a reader and the child must come to understand this and to act upon it.

Whatever the detail, the central idea of gist, and the process of identifying or making it, is one that ties study skills to earlier efforts to construe meanings — for it is an extension of them. The child is likely to need help and there are several ways in which it can be offered. He needs to be helped to make a distinction between local understanding and global understanding. Local understanding is the sometimes temporary sort of understanding that we reach as we work our way through a passage or listen to someone explaining. We feel that we understand, and in a sense we do. We might even be able to answer many comprehension questions on what we have just dealt with. But a longer-term understanding may still be absent. If so, it is probably because we have failed to link up what we have 'understood', *en passant*, with our more permanent knowledge structures. Unless we can do this, we may be in the odd position of both understanding and failing to understand at the same time! Essentially, the reader must learn that in order to come to local understandings, he has to mobilise sufficient knowledge for the purpose; but if his understandings are to be global, he may have to bring other sorts of knowledge to bear. Failure to do this is one reason why the student who works hard at his books nevertheless may seem to have learned little. Often his memory or his intelligence are made scapegoats for what may be no more than inadequate technique.

The search for global meaning and the search for gist go together. Children can be helped in ways already dealt with and also by learning to seek out topic and summarising sentences, by asking questions of the text, both factual and evaluative, such as: what information am I given here, and how important is this information? Highlighting key sentences may help. So might putting in headlines for parts of a text which do not have them.

The process is rather similar to, and is closely linked with, that of making notes. What we said earlier about the purpose of reading and the way that this should be used to govern the sort of reading behaviour that follows applies with equal force to note-making — what is the purpose of the notes? is the main question and the answer should act as a sort of design principle for the subsequent note-taking. Again, there is a danger of an empty 'busyness'. Weighing up the purpose, coming to an understanding, and summarising and filtering that understanding in order to make notes are vastly more important that the actual business of writing them down, for written notes are only the outcroppings of a vast subterranean world. Children need to understand that this process is both normal and inevitable, and that all readers and serious students have to come to terms with it.

Another activity that is closely related to note-making is translation. Translation is what happens when the medium is changed. For example a text dealing with factual matters might be changed into a graph, or a story might become a picture. What must happen is that the similar two-way process to that involved in note-making must be activated. There is first of all the getting of gist together with sufficient detail to suit the purpose behind the enterprise. Then there is the restatement of that gist in whatever form is now sought. Evaluation, in the sense of the reader's estimation of the truth or relevance of what he is reading, plays an important part. It uses criteria and from time to time these criteria should be sought out by the teacher, identified, and examined. The intention is not so much to assist in the comprehension of a particular text, though that may well happen, as to make the reader more conscious of what he is supposed to do in the course of his varied reading activities. There may be the evaluation of data for their significance to local knowledge; there may be the evaluation of local knowledge for its significance to the text that is being read, and there may be evaluation of text and parts of text for their significance to personal learning and so on.

Thus 'study skills' include many diverse but always dynamic

operations, most of them intellectually taxing. The road that children have to travel is a hard one but it is a road down which they can all go. The teacher understands that all the while the child is likely to be close to his own personal frontiers and that the steps he takes are likely to be small ones. I hope that what I have written will help teachers to encourage children to make them and to see that they are in the right direction.

References

Blank, M. (1973) *Teaching Learning in the Pre-School: A Dialogue Approach.* (Columbus, Ohio: Charles E. Merrill)

Kintsch, W. (1972) 'Episodic and Semantic Memory'

Kuhn, T. (1970) *The Structure of Scientific Revolutions*, 2nd edn (Chicago: University of Chicago Press)

Moffett, J. (1968) *Teaching the Universe of Discourse.* (Boston: Houghton Mifflin)

8

The Management of the
Language Policy

Management style

I believe that the management of a school should have two characteristics without which success is impossible: the style of management should be participative; and it should follow some sort of cyclical pattern.

Management is essentially management of the curriculum so when we ask what it is, exactly, that has to be managed there is only one answer that makes real sense. The management of a school is mainly about the curriculum. Matters such as the efficient performance of janitorial duties, the compilation of duty rosters, the organisation of open days, even making arrangements for tea-breaks are all secondary, and themselves only make sense when conducive to curriculum. It is, I think, important to insist upon this for there is a whole world of distraction waiting to divert teachers, and especially heads. The time and energy of the Head and his staff are amongst the most precious commodities in the school; they should not be squandered on anything that is not central to their concerns.

Curriculum

Curriculum itself needs to be seen correctly. It includes all the subject matter that it is hoped children will learn — the maths, the music, the art, their religious knowledge, and so on. But it is much more than this: it has particular relevance for language.

The fact is that much learning simply cannot be prescribed in advance. There are several reasons why this is so. In some areas,

173

the learning that is needed, especially when we talk of the skills, is so multifarious, so involved, and often so delicate, that in real life it is far away from any attempts to delineate it precisely as an aim. As a result, objectives can only be stated at the price of distortion and oversimplification. And yet, ironically, the aim of the proponents of behavioural objectives has always been precision. Classically, such objectives were stated in such a way as to prescribe exactly the learning outcome that was to be achieved and the conditions under which it was to be effected. Thus an objective might run: 'Given a text "A", the student will be able to answer correctly question "B".' But such precision really begs many questions for it does not say what or how the child must learn en route to that objective. For this reason such objectives are spurious and teachers in the United Kingdom have done well on the whole to avoid them. In some cases, objectives have actually been used (for example in primary science) but they have not been couched in such 'precise' behavioural terms. Thus we might have 'Considered that things can change noticeably in length when moved from one position to another.' This is what I should call 'psuedo-behavioural'. It is not precise in stating the conditions under which the action takes place. Nor is it detailed about the 'things' it refers to. Does it mean 'some' or 'all' things? And, of course, some things are too small to be 'noticed' with the eye, in any case. I have no doubt that the attempt to be precise is praiseworthy but the 'precision' often conceals massive learnings or understandings, or applications, that are needed before the target behaviour can be achieved and so the precise detail merely obscures the need for other essential learning.

There is a tradition, founded by Eisner, an American professor of art education, among those who wish to keep to objectives, to admit that, particularly in aesthetic matters, the use of behavioural objectives is inappropriate. Eisner distinguished between instructional objectives that were similar to the old behavioural objectives and 'expressive' objects which were open-ended and which ought to be evaluated by similar techniques to those used in literary or art criticism. He came to advocate what he called 'thick descriptions' based upon an understanding of the complexity of the activity under scrutiny and which took into account such unlikely (to behaviourists) notions as those of purpose and intention. I should like to see this regarded as normal and in no way exceptional. Whilst it is true that such aesthetic outcomes as paintings and poems are always unpredictable because they are open-ended, it is also true that a similar unpredictability attends the so-called 'instructional'

174

outcomes as well. Moreover, in all learning there are antecedent and prerequisite learnings and it is these that must figure as we try to account for individual differences. The result is that an outcome for one child may involve different learning than the same outcome requires for a different child. Objectives, then, distort because they do not do justice either to the depth or to the extent of learning.

So, the notion of curriculum as intended learning is full of difficulties. We are simply not able to be both precise and detailed about it. The concept of unintended learning further complicates the matter. While we can say that the management of the curriculum involves all that contributes to the ordering of teaching and learning, we must add that it includes the building of an ethos in which not only 'prescribed' learning but also, paradoxically, unintended learning can take place. Education is not just about those matters which it is possible to list in advance; it includes learning that we could not normally list, either in advance of its happening because in principal it is impossible to predict, or even after it has happened, because of its complexity. The best we can do is to make some sort of simplifying approximation.

An example might help to bring out the idea of the normalness of this sort of extensive learning. A child who is doing a project on transport may well learn a good deal of what the teacher hopes he will learn. But in doing so he will learn much else as well. The teacher may intend that the child shall end up with a knowledge of the chronology of the development of steam locomotives and of the principles by which they work, but he will also learn vocabulary, a little metallurgy, a notion of expansion and contraction, of pressure, and of the applications of such scientific principles as are involved. This, of course, is all to the good. Such knowledge (which is probably very extensive indeed) is not only steering the child to the desired outcome, it is providing the basis of learning in other spheres as well, some of which may be radically different from the study of locomotives.

At the same time the child may become more interested in, and more knowledgeable about, the remarkable Stephensons, father and son, whose characters seem to have had as much to do with their success in engineering as did their grasp of technology. Again, such learning is all to the good — but it is not necessarily encompassed in stated objectives. Nor is this sort of factual learning the only sort that may have been unintended. Where the atmosphere is right the child may find himself encouraged to do what is one of the most difficult things in the whole of his career as a learner and that is to ask himself questions — a procedural ploy of great potency and one which adds to the dimension of depth. It is of course possible that the school may intend that he shall do just that. But even so there is an essential open-endedness about the process. The questions that one child asks will not necessarily be the same or have the same depth as those that another child asks.

There is a third area where some, at least, of the learning will not be intended, mainly because learning there is usually effected informally and indirectly. This is the realm of 'attitudes', which was dealt with in the last chapter. Attitudes are ways of 'looking' at things that incorporate within themselves values as a major component. In learning to have consideration for others, children are likely to learn as much from examples, whether intended or not, and from reading and drama, as they are from direct homily. Moreover, though homilies can be timed and thus prescribed, much attitude learning is actually unwitting. For instance, children's self-esteem, at least within the boundaries of school life is an image formed by successful or unsuccessful encounters with problems of learning and with experiencing the feeling that they themselves are valued, especially by people who are powerful or for whom they have high regard. For a school to prescribe such outcomes, still less to design the teaching and learning that would inevitably bring them on, is simply not possible. The matter is too complex, the children too different from one another, and the learning too informal.

Although, therefore, there are areas of the curriculum where learning is 'unintended', or at least unprescribed, this does not mean that the school can do nothing about them. Indeed, since such learning is amongst the most important learning that the child will ever do — important in the example above in personality development and vital in the matter of motivation — the school cannot afford to ignore it. Its way of tackling it must be very largely to concern itself with the sort of ethos that it constitutes, with the sort of environment and context for learning that it creates, and with the values, especially in regard to humans, that it exemplifies. In these respects the curriculum is very wide indeed and language — to return for a moment to our ultimate concern — flows into and out of every part of it.

Participative management

The conviction that management ought to be participatory in style and method was first aired in Chapter 1. The reasons for it are practical, both educationally and politically. Educationally, it makes for effectiveness. Politically, particularly when it includes responsibility for the curriculum amongst its main concerns, it serves to place curriculum decisions where they belong — with teachers. Perhaps the overriding consideration is that unless there is participation when decisions are made, there is unlikely to be proper implementation when those decisions are put into effect. In this respect, participation means *full* participation. It will not do, for example for the Head to send off his language specialist or any other member of staff, to a few courses and then expect him or her on return to write a curriculum policy document even if that document were then to be put before staff for their approval. Participation is a process and is not merely a formal requirement.

When we pause to consider the links between participation and proper implementation, between the planning of a policy and carrying it out, we realise that participation leads to, and is sometimes a condition of, commitment. Teachers who are not committed have excellent opportunities of going slow, of defusing or ignoring or even of sabotaging decisions. More charitably, if they have not participated in the full process, they may not have come to see the need for any change that might be called for, or to develop the knowledge and skills necessary for that change to be made successfully, even if they had seen the need for it in the first place.

Participation means that there will be full discussion and this discussion gives the manager many golden opportunities. He can make sure that the need for change or review will be broached and aired and that any proposed planning process is outlined to his staff so that everyone is in the picture. Discussion, as we shall see later, is important, too, in the development of staff expertise. Above all, though, discussion is a process which allows the staff to operate as a staff, which involves give and take, which allows all to learn and all to teach by contributing. It brings about a new sort of openness in education. We have had so-called 'open schools' and 'open education' for a long time. Now the call is for an openness which says, in effect,

We teachers, members of this school, are in a certain responsible and caring relationship to each other. Our expertise is at each other's disposal. Much that elsewhere might be private, we bring into our mutual domain. We discuss our difficulties; we are pleased to be helped to strengthen our weaknesses. We take responsibility collectively and can justify the process by which we do so.

When we reach such openness, I have no doubt that the result will be happier and immensely more effective schools.

Cyclical planning

It is very much in line with the idea of participatory management that the planning of any part of the curriculum should be cyclical. This means using something like a PIE-model, 'PIE' standing for 'Planning', 'Implementing' and 'Evaluating' (see p. 4). An important feature is that the planning stage includes planning for both implementing and evaluating the effectiveness of what has been planned and taught.

Cyclical planning is characteristic of the school which believes that all in it have much to learn and that much of what the teachers have to learn is how to improve their own work. The notion of evaluation is one which implies very strongly that the school's work is unlikely ever to be perfect, that it is subject to review, that the staff intend to learn from their experiences and that, given participative discussion, they will learn also from each other's experiences.

Of course, in practice, matters will not be as clear-cut as the model suggests. Evaluation is, in some sense, going on all the time. It would be wrong for teachers utterly to postpone judgements of any kind on their work and its effectiveness until the season for evaluation had approached. Monitoring, the taking of feedback, the modification of approaches, even the alteration of process and content, should not await any 'official' time for evaluating. What should happen when that time comes is that the original plans, any modifications made to them, and the whole process of the application of those plans in practice should be discussed with a view to improving them before the cycle begins its next round.

What the language policy document might contain: the sections

Our present concern is with planning that will take the form of a language policy. Here we shall move ahead to consider again what the language policy document might look like. Once this is done, we shall return to consider the roles of the Head, the language consultant, members of staff, and others in the PIE process.

It is possible to operate a language policy without having a written document, for what a school actually does *is* the policy. But, if the argument advanced earlier has substance, there are powerful reasons why it should take a written form. If this is agreed, the next practical question to be answered is: what exactly should a language policy document contain? I do not believe that there can be a single answer to that question. Much will depend on the scale on which a particular school wants to plan, and perhaps on the existence of other plans. For example there may be a pre-existing set of guidelines for reading that a school may wish to incorporate into its policy with as little change as possible. For the purpose of illustration, however, I shall assume that we are dealing with the needs of a school that wishes to plan and to write out its language policy in full.

Even in such circumstances, there are several options open. The main requirement is, I believe, that it should be comprehensive — that it should cover all the major matters to do with language. The problem then becomes one of identifying these. When this is done, it is very possible to treat each part of the policy shortly or at great length. Other important questions then require an answer. How far should the document deal with principles? To what extent should it deal with methods? Ought it to sketch in at least the salient features of children's development in the various skills? Should the document recommend, or even list resources?

Judging from experience, I do not think that it is possible for a school finally to answer all these questions in advance. Very often, significance only becomes apparent when one gets immersed in the business. What one can do is to start with certain intentions, knowing that they are necessarily tentative and that they can be changed as discussions go on. With this qualification in mind, it is quite possible to suggest certain rather minimal requirements that all 'comprehensive' policy documents ought to meet.

Another procedural question that the school will have to settle is whether the document will be sectionalised according to the age of the child or with regard to developmental status. There could be, for example, a section on 'reading in the infant years' and another on 'reading in the junior years'. I am not convinced that this would not be a mistake. We ought to be able to take it for granted that, whatever the outcome, the finished document ought to be as useful to teachers in the junior years as it is to those in the infant years. Whatever arrangement is made, there is everything to be said for all the staff helping to shape, and thereby subscribe to, all the language work of the school.

Each member of staff can learn from the others. As a particular example, many teachers of older juniors have, I think, a great deal to learn from their infant colleagues about reading. Essentially, I believe, the document should deal with developmental progression and it is this that needs to be emphasised. Reading, to go back to our example, does not become different in the junior years. Further, the language skills need to be seen in two ways — each in its entirety and all together in their interdependence. Accordingly, I should advocate, 'all through' sections which take each of the skills right through the primary range. I would, however, wish to qualify this somewhat with regard to early literacy. For reasons which are explained elsewhere, I believe that the transition stage to literacy is highly distinctive and that this is true whether an individual is making the transition as an infant, a junior, or even as an adult.

With such considerations in mind, I would suggest that schools might consider adopting the following arrrangement:

(1)   speaking and listening;
(2)   the transition to literacy;
(3)   the development of reading;
(4)   the development of writing;
(5)   language in learning and across the curriculum.

This is comprehensive in that it caters for all the major skills and for the place of language in the school as a whole as well as in the life of the individual learner. But there are still some questions to settle. Where will handwriting come? Ought it to be dealt with at all in a *language* policy? If it is to be included, the best place will probably be in section (2) and again at greater length in section (4).

What about literature? Is it really good enough to subsume this under 'the development of reading'? I believe that it is and that it would be a great mistake to cut it off from other matters to do with learning to read. After all, when children are learning to read, they are supposed to be learning to read literature among other things. The importation of the notion of 'mechanical skills' of reading into schools, affecting as it does the approaches that teachers adopt and the materials that they buy for children, has, I am sure, been a complete disaster. I do not believe that such skills exist. Be that as it may, and in case there is any doubt, let me say that I want to put 'literature' in the reading section because I value it so highly and not because I am seeking to relegate it in any way to an inferior status.

Drama is another sphere which might be included in a language policy. There is no doubt that drama, and with it play, affords valuable and unique opportunities to children. These are by no means confined to language, but both play and drama are excellent means of developing speaking and listening skills. Should they be included in the language policy, or should they be dealt with elsewhere? It is difficult to conceive of a language policy that does not recognise and commend their importance. To this extent, at least, both belong in the policy document. It would also be possible to have separate guidelines for each if a school wished to develop its ideas further and especially if it wished to bring out aspects of play and drama that are not specifically or mainly linguistic — though, as the reader will be aware, the proper sphere of the linguistic is itself very wide.

I suggest above that the transition to literacy should be treated as a separate section. The reasons emerge from the discussion of that phase in this book. In brief, they are that the phase is special in degree because of the extraordinarily intimate relationship between all four skills at that stage, and, secondarily, that transitional reading is different in kind from 'true' reading, though the idea is to get the two gradually to merge. A further advantage of treating the stage separately is that it should help those colleagues who have to deal with 'remedial' cases in the junior years. Remedial reading is, alas, noted for its lack of success. I believe that some of the reasons for this lie in the wish, which in itself is entirely understandable and commendable, of the junior teacher that her remedial child should make rapid progress back to normality. Unfortunately, this too often leads away from a truly developmental view. The trouble afflicting a backward junior — a child with 'special needs' — may be not so much that he is dim at making phonic analyses and blends as that he has not acquired enough written language through the ear by being read to to allow him to cope with the printed version. It is this sort of consideration that points to the need to deal with the interdependence of the language skills.

What the sections of the document might contain

The aim in formulating a language policy must be to combine comprehensiveness with succinctness. A policy is not so much a treatise as it is a set of guidelines. If the guidelines are to be useful to the reader, we must ask what their characteristic content ought to be. Whatever the answer may turn out to be, it should be as brief as possible, or else it may not be read at all.

In making suggestions for what are really the subheadings of the sections, I should mention that what is suggested is usually only one among a range of possibilities. But, further, it seems to me that unless these are included, the document will fall short of what is needed.

Goals and outcomes

Here the question of behavioural objectives will crop up — and it must be decided whether they are appropriate goals in any part of the language programme. Behavioural objectives, it will be recalled, are those which specify exactly what a learner will be able to do and under what conditions, if there has been successful, intended, learning. By their nature they are detailed, but the canvas of language learning is so wide that if we were to attempt to couch all our ends in such behavioural terms, we should have an unmanageable plethora on our hands.

Consequently because of these and other reasons which have been discussed earlier, it is, I think, preferable to think throughout in terms not of the destinations which children must reach, but of directions in which they ought to go. Probably, too, there should be emphasis on the breadth and depth of what they must also learn in order to travel. To examine such antecedent and prerequisite learning has been, of course, a major purpose of this book. At this point an example might be useful. Instead of using a behavioural objective, we might say that our aim in reading is to get the child to construe different sorts of meaning from different sorts of texts and to employ a range of appropriate techniques as he does so. Here we have a broad aim which is useful in emphasising that the essential feature of reading is that it is a process concerned with getting meaning from texts, that there are both different sorts of meanings and different sorts of texts and that the problem for children is to acquire and employ techniques suitable for dealing with them. It is true that the phrase 'getting meaning from texts' may not accurately define the process by which meaning is construed but the idea can be further refined in the document. Writing this part of the policy in the way suggested does not yet define precisely what the teacher must do but it sets her well on the right path, heading in the right direction. The rest of the skills can be treated in a broadly similar way.

Approaches and methods

It would be a great mistake to suppose that, once the main ends have been agreed, methods and techniques can be left to the individual teacher; to believe that there needs only to be collective agreement about the big things, but that details, such as techniques, should be purely within the private province of the class teacher. The truth is that once the goals are agreed, they act as a powerful constraint on the choices that are then left. For example, it is clear that very young children, such as those of nursery and pre-nursery years, need to go through a process of learning to speak and to listen in partnership with a skilled and empathetic expert in speaking and listening — in practice usually their mother or a teacher. If so, this puts a powerful bind on what a school can do with such a child. It must either lay on such encounters, or admit that it cannot do so. It will not suffice to hope that a child will achieve the skilled ease and fluency that he really needs simply by being in a good atmosphere, or by playing with his peers, or even by listening to stories or living in a linguistic environment that in all other respects is rich, for what he needs, principally, is an adult to relate to and to converse with.

The same applies to other skills. Each imposes certain constraints upon the teacher. Reading for example, requires the teacher not merely to pursue her own path but to identify what techniques children have to learn to become fully competent and then to judge when the time is ripe and the materials appropriate for such learning. One important skill which children must learn, for instance, is to form expectations about the meaning that they are construing from the text. It follows from this that the texts from which they are working should be the sort that allow such expectations to be formed. This would put them in sharp contrast to certain primers whose texts jump about incoherently and which in this way are fiercely counter-productive.

We could take another example from writing. Here, the goals

must, I think, include that of 'putting' meaning into appropriate structures. For example, the genre may influence the choice of grammatical structure. A poster may not need sentences, especially for its headings. Writing a shopping list or a timetable may also require structures that are not sentences. There is no doubt, however, that the appropriate structural vehicle for most writing is the sentence. It follows that children must at some time learn to write sentences and to distinguish sentences from non-sentences and, further, that they must learn to write in a variety of sentence structures according to the purposes for which they are writing and the meanings they are trying to communicate. They must learn which structure, from all their repertoire, is most appropriate to the task in hand. Learning such matters is a long job — one that probably never really ends. But there is, I think, no doubt that the child should be on this particular road. The teacher, accordingly, needs to devise approaches, methods and tasks that will help. It will not do to ignore the problem or to suppose, as the proponents of creative writing seemed to, that if the child is motivated and excited by a stimulating task, all the rest of the necessary learning would inevitably follow. Interesting writing tasks there must be, but a moment's thought is enough to convince anyone that an interesting task cannot in itself account for all the learning that needs to take place. What about the child's experience of other people's written sentences, for instance? Are examples brought to his notice at appropriate moments? Is he being congratulated on being able to write a sentence of the '. . . and . . . and . . . and . . . ' type early in his career and is he then encouraged to try new methods of combining and joining as new ways of conveying meaning when these are appropriate? How many of the strategies suggested in Chapter 5 are actually being used?

The truth may be that getting from broad goals and principles into methods and materials that are appropriate to a particular child's needs at a particular stage in his development is one of the hardest tasks in teaching. It certainly calls for considerable knowledge and insight on the part of the teacher. But it is not a matter that can ever be decided in the absence of agreed goals and these will provide both opportunities and limitations on what can legitimately be tried.

Writers of a language policy are thus faced with a considerable difficulty, for it will not be possible to specify all the techniques, methods or materials that will be useful. What could be done is first to establish the principle that they should all be compatible with the goals and capable of furthering them. Then the document could go on to give examples of some that are among the more important.

Even when that is done, this will be the exact area in which some colleagues will need most help when the time comes to implement the policy. The fact that one may subscribe wholeheartedly to attaining certain goals does not mean that the methods for doing so will necessarily become obvious or available. Colleagues, and especially the language consultant, have a role here and subsequent staff discussions can be used to pool ideas. Once members of staff feel the need to explore this area, they become stronger. When they realise that there are broad purposes that can be stated with some clarity and that these then create certain needs as far as methods and materials are concerned, they have a powerful scanning device which they can use when they visit school, attend courses, or read books. It enables them to acquire the riches and reject the dross. It is, no doubt a cliche, but the good teacher is always a good learner.

Records

It is probably a very sound sentiment in teachers which makes them suspicious of anything that does not contribute directly to the business of teaching and learning. Records and record-keeping have often excited suspicion on this score. While they are necessary, it is felt, rightly I think, that they can so often get out of hand and become an end in themselves. Alternatively, they can seem to be irrelevant. Many records exist that are never consulted by the teachers for whom they are supposed to be a help. Accordingly, it seems useful to ask that records shall only be kept with a definite purpose, useful to teachers, in mind.

In what follows I shall ignore mandatory records — those which local authorities insist must be kept — unless they are valid for other reasons. Similarly, I shall pay no attention to those which are supposed to facilitate transfer between nursery school and infant school and between infant school and junior school. Such records are, of course, unnecessary in the all-through primary school which I am taking as my example. Neither shall I discuss records for the transfer to secondary school, as such. Nevertheless what is said below ought to have some relevance in all these areas.

Records should, I believe, follow the principle of parsimony, being as brief as possible and used only for agreed, specific purposes. Further, this purpose ought to dictate the sort of record that is kept. Within these limitations, there are two sorts of record that might be useful — those that the individual teacher needs and those that the school needs to ensure continuity and to help in the evaluation of the work. The first sort might be nobody's business but her own. Many 'records' of this kind will be kept in her head or in documents of her own devising — sometimes they will be very rough and ready. Their justification is their usefulness in helping the teacher to foster the child's development consistently and coherently. She will certainly need, for example, records of every child's current reading. Sometimes the best person, by far, to keep such a record will be the child himself. As far as spoken language is concerned, the teacher will need some note of whether the child is still in the position of learning mainly through conversation with an adult, or whether he can now be left more to interactions with his peers, and whether he can attempt longer utterances, and, if so, in what circumstances, and in regard to what subject matter. If these records are personal to the teacher, there is no need for them to be in prescribed form or to be communicable to other teachers.

I am far from decrying the subjective, the overall, or the non-statistical judgement in keeping these records. How a child's progress appears to the teacher, what his present status as a learner is, and where he probably needs to go next are matters of cardinal importance. The teacher's opinions in these respects ought never to be endangered by the demands of 'posh' record sheets which are sometimes seen to be designed to be impressive and which often turn out to be inane.

Nor should I wish to diminish the teacher's judgements as far as the non-private school records are concerned. They, too, should be in keeping with the dictum that records should always have acceptable purposes and they should be designed with these purposes in mind. What, then, can be said about such purposes? I see two and am reluctant to admit any others. The first is to enable the school to evaluate the whole or part of its language work; the second is to enable the school to monitor the progress of each child, to ensure continuity in his teaching and learning from year to year.

Records that are suitable for these purposes may well differ in kind as they relate to different parts of the language work. In connection with writing, I have already suggested that the most appropriate record might take the form of a file for each child in which samples of his writing are kept, together with a commentary from the teacher. Collecting such material is easy. The hard part is in saying what it is evidence of. Appearances count, of course. The psychomotor aspects of writing will be the most apparent, and over a period of time there will be clear evidence of whether or not the child is increasing his ability to handwrite and to control the general layout and presentation of his writing. Next, what we might call the surface aspects of the composition will be most accessible. These include spelling, punctuation and 'correct' grammar. They are not unimportant, of course. But it is possible to make the mistake of regarding them as 'it'. Critics outside schools, such as employers, are often fixated at this level. Essentially, if it goes no further, it is an ignorant person who assumes that this is the heart of the matter — it is a bit like saying that a man who is dying has a poor complexion. What we must look after includes these surface features but goes much deeper. Our job, and the child's too, is much more extensive and in this way more difficult than is sometimes supposed. And so, the commentary kept with the samples might include those matters which were dealt with in Chapter 6 — matters, among others, of the 'independence' of a child's writing, of sequencing, sentence structure, cohesion and coherence and so on.

The same records will often do for both the purposes we designated. Commentaries on a child's writing are not only useful for helping a particular child. They help, at the end of a period when we look back, to provide the evidence by which we can evaluate the programme. Here again, what matters is the professional judgement of the teachers. I do not believe that in any there are any valid norms or averages by which the progress of a child, still less the worth of a language policy or the effectiveness of a school, can legitimately be judged.

Evaluation

Evaluation needs to be discussed at the same time as the policy is formulated. Staff may then come to see various problems. One difficulty to be avoided is lack of balance. If there is tension between the claims of teaching and those of evaluation, it is better to teach. Nevertheless it is, as I have insisted, arrogant not to wish to evaluate. To evaluate is to declare that further improvements are possible.

Evaluation itself can be global and impressionistic. A teacher's verdict on a policy or on part of it will be founded on a multitude of impressions gained mainly informally over a period of time.

These will be measured against some criteria that the teacher has made her own and these criteria are vital. If any sort of summing up is to be made for the whole staff, it is as well that the criteria used by different teachers should be made explicit and comparable. And so, one of the most important tasks that can be done at the planning stage is to look forward to try to identify the criteria that will eventually be used. These ought to be realistic and usable, but as time goes on they should eventually become more rigorous.

Not all the evidence will be impressionistic. For example, it would be quite possible to count the number of books read in a class over a period and to compare this with the number read in a later similar period. This would give evidence of reading appetite, at least. Set tests might also be used, but these do not easily fit in with the views of competence I have expressed.

One good way into evaluation is to ascertain what departures have been made from the policy, the degree of change involved, and to estimate the probable effectiveness of the changes. Teachers and the staff as a whole have not only a right but a duty to make alterations if they think that some part of the policy is not working properly. It should be understood, however, that the Head or the language consultant must be informed. Such changes themselves indicate a sort of evaluation. They need to be discussed fully and the opinions of staff need to be sought.

Finally, it might be useful to deal with the distinction between 'formative' and 'summative' evaluation. The latter is a process which tries to make judgements about the effectiveness of a programme, once that programme is completed. Its purpose might possibly be to determine whether a scheme, say of curriculum development, has or has not been successful. Personally, I can see little point in this sort of evaluation, at least in connection with the PIE-model. 'Formative' evaluation, on the other hand is aimed at improving whatever is being evaluated. It sees implementing and evaluating as ongoing processes and thus lends itself to the PIE cycle that we have been advocating and which looks backward in order to look forward.

The interrelatedness of skills

Each section of a language policy should explore, at least in outline, the interrelatedness of the skills. Understanding this gives us one of the main reasons why we should have a language policy in the first place. Literacy depends, for example, on a previous mastery of spoken language. That is not to say that a person who has no spoken language could not learn to read and write. What it means is that, in our culture, when normal people attain literacy they always exploit the immense knowledge of the spoken language that has been gained through the ear and by speaking. Nor is it merely knowledge of the spoken language that is gained in this way, for one of the hopeful aspects of literacy learning is that a great deal of knowledge of written language can also be gained through the ear. In other words, a continuing programme of speaking and listening development is a necessary condition for the successful learning of reading and writing. I say 'continuing' because it is not a matter of 'doing' speaking and listening up to the point where reading and writing take over. The child will go on increasing the resources which fit him to become a more competent reader and writer through the knowlege that comes to him through the speech programme. The same is true in reverse. After a time, a child begins to acquire knowledge of language through reading and, to a lesser extent, through writing, which will begin to affect further his progress in speaking and listening. He will meet sentences galore and some of them will have quite specialised structures which may be fairly rare in speech. But though rare, they will be perfectly usable — at appropriate times.

Some of these points are taken further in the sections of this book which deal with the different skills. The important point for the manager is to insist that because of this interrelatedness it is not acceptable to have only, for example, a reading policy. The intimate connections of reading with writing and with learning to speak and to listen must be stressed because it is in them that the conditions for success or failure in reading often lie.

Roles

One of the more useful importations that we can make from management theory is the insistence that in any organisation roles should be defined and generally understood. What follows in this chapter is an attempt to delineate some of the principal roles that must be played in the process of formulating, implementing and evaluating a language policy.

189

The Head

It may surprise some to contemplate the fact that in the enterprise of making a language policy the language consultant plays what is a vital but nevertheless minor role. In comparison with that of the Head, it is secondary in importance. The Head's role will be considered first for it is his role and the nature of the enterprise that, to a large extent, define the roles of the other participants.

Once the possibility of replanning language work becomes serious, whether because of sentiments inside the school or of advice from outside, the Head needs to begin by getting for himself an understanding of what language is and how it is learned. Numbers of books, including this one, have been written to help him, and the various language course materials of the Open University are well worth scrutiny. He needs to be careful that he comes to an understanding which does justice to the relationship of language learning to other sorts of learning and which takes in the relationships among the various language skills that children must learn. He can also ask his language consultant for help, though there is much to be said for coming to an independent understanding.

Once he feels he knows his way around the field, the question of whether the school should in fact proceed to replan its language work becomes more realistic. If he considers that the school should go ahead, there are two tasks he must then undertake. The first is to come to some sort of rough estimate of the sort of replanning that he intends. Is it to be of the whole of the language policy? Is it to concentrate on part of it? Is it to be a thorough exercise or, in all the circumstances (some of which will have nothing to do with language but will reflect the other concerns of the school), will it be more cursory? These questions can only be answered tentatively, for the planning process cannot be forecast with complete accuracy. What can and should be fixed is a time limit on the work. And so the Head needs, after talking to individuals, to go to his staff to advocate the idea that the staff should undertake this sort of curriculum planning and at the same time he should try to give some idea of the depth of the enterprise and a clearer idea of how long a time should be allocated to it. This idea of a time limit is a practical necessity. There are schools who have, to my knowledge, been formulating a language policy for years and the desire to get it perfect has caused them to postpone its completion and eventually to flounder irresolutely. At this point the agreement of the staff is essential.

190

Once the agreement of the staff is secured, more detailed work can begin. The planning of a language policy itself requires planning and this is the Head's responsibility. The arrangement of meetings, the allocation of clerical assistance, the nomination of people to take the lead in parts of the enterprise are functions that he must undertake though he may take advice and often will welcome volunteers. The point is that unless time limits are set and people given responsibility, and unless progress is chased pretty rigorously, the whole process may become becalmed. Such arrangements need to be approved by the staff as a whole but the main dynamic factor is still the Head. That is why we say that participative styles need a strong Head.

Probably the most effective way to proceed is by having small study and drafting groups working on different parts of the policy. Very often members of staff may be on more than one such group (which may meet successively ran than contemporaneously). There is no need for the Head to be a member of more than the odd one. Probably, the language consultant will work with several such groups. In principle, groups should include both members of staff with special interests and those who have no such special concerns. If the division into areas and sections that was recommended earlier is adopted, there will be no question of, for example, infant language work being planned solely by a group of infant teachers. Each of the areas should have staff who normally teach the younger as well as the older children.

Groups need guidelines to work to and these guidelines, which again need to be discussed in full staff meeting, might be drawn up by the Head and the language consultant together. If a group is to plan, say the work in speaking and listening then, in addition to its expertise in fostering language development, it needs to know:

(1) the deadline by which it must produce its draft;
(2) the length of its draft;
(3) how that draft might be sectionalised — for example will there be a section outlining the salient features of development? Will there be a section dealing with goals and if so in what form? Will there be sections devoted to approaches, methods, evaluation, marking policy, the role of parents and so on? How far should the draft attempt to link up with development in other areas — how far, that is, should it look into the notion of the interrelatedness of skills? Should it attempt to list resources, or to make any recommendations about them?

These are not easy questions to answer, and it may be that some of the guidance has to be given tentatively, subject to later change. The point is that without such guidance, planning and drafting are difficult and relatively aimless.

Drafts, once delivered, need careful scrutiny by the Head and his consultant. There needs to be some comparability between one section and another. There must be no omissions. The balance within a section needs to be right. Above all, what is written may have serious implications for other parts of the policy or for the school as a whole. For example, there may be implied consequences for resources. The planning process, therefore, should be well understood in advance to include this sort of scrutiny before a draft goes to the full staff. It may well be necessary for the Head or the consultant to take a draft back to its group to resolve any difficulties that have arisen.

The approval of drafts by the full staff is an essential step and one which needs to be very carefully managed. The main considera-tion is that there should be no question of 'rubber stamping'. There may be a temptation to say that the drafting group has done a good and thorough job — one which clearly has won the approval and even the admiration of the rest of the staff, with the result that their work can be taken as read. If this were to happen, it would be a great pity, for what the Head and his staff are really engaged upon is a twin enterprise of curriculum and staff development. One makes no sense without the other. Staff meetings to discuss curriculum development are themselves exercises in staff development. That is why the draft, when it reaches the staff, should be regarded as a discussion document. Policy documents tend to be drafted at a fairly high level of generalisation. At the highest levels, principles of development and matters of the relationships between the parts need to be expounded for the benefit of members of staff who need to extend their own understandings. Below that level of generality, there is a gradual broadening into matters that are strictly practical. Marking policy is an example which links practical considerations to deeply theoretical considerations. How is children's written work to be received? How is it to be marked? Is all written work to be marked the same way? What is the staff's attitude to errors? Is there any place for numerical marks or grades? How are records of a child's work to be kept? How will work in that part of the language policy eventually be evaluated? What is the most profitable use of the teacher's time in connection with the children's writing? Is there already enough expertise in the school or should outsiders be called in, visits made, courses attended, and books read?

From this it is clear that the wise head should have as much regard for the process of forming a language policy as he will for the eventual product. He is dealing with the making of teachers and with the building of a school.

Even a strong Head who is running sound processes may still be faced with difficulties that seem insuperable. What, for example, should be done about teachers who are unwilling to go along with collective decisions and who claim the right to go their own way? They may be motivated by real conviction, or their refusal to cooperate may be a reflection of their own discontent, inadequacy or bloody-mindedness. I think it is essential that they should be drawn into the planning process. Further, it should be explained to them that they will be expected to implement what the staff as a whole eventually decide. If they refuse, they should be offered the chance to write their own dissenting policy on a similar scale to that adopted by the staff. In other words a price should be paid for contracting out and it should be that the schemes of work they wish to implement should be as well thought out and presented as the rest of the language policy. Any such dissenting documents could be attached to the language policy itself, perhaps with comments on its adequacy made by the Head. There is, it seems to me, no absolute reason why dissent should not be tolerated. But dissent should not be a path to lesser effort or inferior preparation.

This brings us back again to the question of the ethos or climate of the school. Ultimately it is the responsibility of the Head. He does not, however, usually create it in the first place. Unless he is in a new school, he inherits it. If he is faced with the result of neglect or of outworn styles of management, he has gradually to move the school into new ways of working and cooperating. This is never easy and some Heads become discouraged by any initial lack of success. There often seems to be in a school one or two teachers, sometimes of considerable seniority or even antiquity, whose personalities send out the message that they are not to be trifled with, that their work is satisfactory, that they know that it is and that change is not for them. Further, given the demographic and economic changes of recent times, all heads are going to have to face extra problems of ageing staffs, with decreased mobility and poorer prospects of even modest promotion. Staff have more cause nowadays to become cynical or disgruntled. There is one powerful factor which mitigates much of this — while creating, it must be admitted, new problems: it is that primary schools are getting smaller. Generally speaking, the smaller the school the easier it is to manage personal relationships because size makes for remoteness and can lead to alienation.

In these circumstances, when so many opportunities are denied to them, staff need to find compensation in job satisfaction. The idea that they are enhancing their own professional competence; that, consequently their children are going to have better prospects than they would otherwise have had; the sense that they belong to an organisation — a community — that is working well and is itself seeking to make progress — such matters will become even more important in the future than they have been in the past. Again, the leadership role of the Head is vital. The situation both presents opportunities to improve schools and imposes limits on what can be done.

Finally, we look ahead to the later phases of the planning cycle. The pressing need, once the policy is in operation, is to see that it is in fact being implemented. Here the language consultant, who should be in close touch with what is actually happening in each classroom, will be a valuable ally. If the policy is not being implemented the reason must be ascertained. It could be one of several reasons, some blameworthy, such as neglect or indifference, some praiseworthy like a late conviction that some part of it seems to be unworkable in practice. The Head should act accordingly. Much the most likely reason, however, is likely to be in the area of professional competence — the skills of translating general principles into concrete day-by-day actions may not be adequate to meet the new needs. Here there is a continuing role for the language consultant in offering help.

There is another sphere in which the Head needs to act. The business of replanning language work is, of course, an exercise in innovation. Innovation is dangerous in the sense that it may alarm those who are not convinced of its value. Parents, time and time again, have shown their concern when faced with changes, particularly in reading, that they do not support. Some schools have, indeed, had to cope with an unholy alliance between anxious parents and reactionary members of staff. Now, there is surely a golden rule about innovation in school. It is that parents should be kept informed from as early as possible and that every reasonable step is taken to explain the reasons for, and nature of, the proposed change. This may involve meetings, letters, brochures or other means of communication. Schools owe it to parents to explain and thus to reassure them. And schools simply cannot afford to allow parents to drift through neglect into opposition and hostility.

The language consultant's role

The language consultant's role is of course very important, but the consultant is not the Head and the major role is the Head's. Accordingly, this description of what the consultant needs to know and to do has to be understood in the framework set by the role of the Head.

Perhaps the most important insight of all that the consultant needs is an understanding of the implications of changes in language work. Earlier, we noted two important two-way relationships. The first was between language and human relationships in the school. Language profoundly affects and is profoundly affected by such relationships, especially those between teachers and children. Similarly, the whole of the curriculum gives opportunity for the use and learning of language — and language makes much of the curriculum accessible, even in areas that are not themselves principally verbal. Mathematics is not itself, for example, a verbal subject in the same way as, say, history or religious studies. Nevertheless, when it comes to the learning and teaching of mathematics, language has an important instrumental role.

Language, then, has far-reaching implications for every aspect of the school's work and life and cannot be partitioned into a corner. Accordingly, the consultant must explore these implications and in doing so will need to employ a great deal of tact and to tread warily, for there is no single toe that she might not tread on. This is not the end of the complications, of course, because another powerful insight is that the language skills are themselves interrelated and, as each depends upon and furthers the others, it is impossible to make changes in any part of the language work without affecting all the other parts. Thus, innovation in language has particularly powerful reverberations and can be handled properly only by those who are prepared to take a comprehensive view of all that is involved

No doubt such considerations should be prominent in the mind of the Head and the consultant as they decide to recommend the planning or replanning of a language policy. Whether they go ahead is of course a matter of priorities: it cannot be decided with reference to language alone but must take into account the other concerns of the school and the history of any recent changes in language or elsewhere in the curriculum. Once it is decided to go ahead, the consultant needs to help the Head in first of all persuading other members of staff of the need to be agreed, at least provisionally. Without this sort of planning of the planning, many unnecessary difficulties may grow, for it may be that deadlines operate as a necessary spur. Like imminent execution, they help to concentrate the mind wonderfully.

It is likely that the work of studying and drafting will fall to small groups of staff. If so, a member of the group should be asked to make a draft for later presentation to staff meeting. This will require accurate records of what transpires at each planning meeting. At each session, the records of the previous meeting should be reviewed. This helps to secure continuity and to make it clear what exactly is up for discussion and decision. Both this discussion and the later drafting will need a great deal of guidance and here the Head and the consultant need to give help on length, format and probable content, as was discussed above.

The consultant cannot help to give such guidance unless she is clear about certain matters. She needs to know exactly what sections the policy document will be divided into, and also what each section might contain. She will need to be clear about the way in which objectives or goals, or other outcomes are to be framed. There must eventually be some uniformity among the different sections in this regard. This, too, was discussed above. Whether or not she agrees with the conclusions there, it is important that she knows her own mind and that of the Head. They need agreement and they need absolute clarity before they can recommend a particular course of action to their colleagues.

Once preliminary drafting begins, the consultant must be available to advise the various groups. She will have an overview, she will see the larger context into which all must eventually fit. She will, in all probability, have a wider knowledge of approaches and materials than most of her colleagues. She will know when a group runs into difficulties and she can thus suggest helpful procedures. She will come to know when members of staff lack expertise or confidence and she can then help, for example by reassuring them or by arranging visits, or by making books available.

Once a group has made its draft it can then be discussed by the full staff. At this point, discussion rather than decision is the aim. If there is radical disagreement, the draft may need to go back to the group; if not, or if only relatively minor modifications are needed, it can become the reponsibility of the consultant to make them and to report back to the full staff for approval. The final drafting of the whole document should be the work of one person and there are really only two candidates for the job — the Head and the consultant. On the whole it is better that the consultant should do it. As she does, she needs to look to such matters as consistency in format, style and type of content. She needs to think about the implications of each section for the others and for the school as a whole. Above all, she needs to believe that process is at least as important as product: that the making of the policy is even more important than the document itself.

One part of the policy which it is perhaps inherently more difficult to manage satisfactorily than the rest is that part which deals with language in individual learning and across the curriculum. As we have pointed out, it also has implications for human relations, but as far as areas of the curriculum are concerned, a great deal of cooperation will be needed with staff who have responsibility for, or who are interested in, these areas. They, too, need to understand what their areas can do for language development and also how far their work there depends on language. In order to come to such understandings there must be clarity about the ends of learning and about the ways such learning is effected. Accordingly, the section of the document that deals with these matters will present certain challenges. One way forward is to invite those interested to contribute notes which deal with their own special concerns. These could then be compared and discussed. In view of the special difficulties involved, the best course might be for the consultant to take responsibility for all drafting in this area. She will need to keep the Head closely informed, to make sure that he is aware of the issues and that he is encouraged to lend his influence to getting members of staff to contribute and to furthering the discussions and thus adding to each other's understandings.

When the policy comes to be implemented, the consultant needs to be in constant discussion with members of staff, talking about ways of teaching and taking note of any special difficulties which might have implications for in-service training or for the eventual modification of the policy. There is much to be said for lightening her own teaching commitments so that she can do this and also so that she can go into classrooms and teach side-by-side with other members of staff. How far she can be freed to take on such functions, is, of course, a matter for the Head operating within the staffing constraints imposed by his education authority.

The overall purpose of the language policy is, of course, that every child both should extend his linguistic competence and use this in further learning. Records are essential for this purpose.

The language consultant needs constantly to scrutinise such records in order to see that each child is making at least satisfactory progress. Discussing every child and his record with his class teacher should be an important part of her role. General surveys of classes, global impressions of schools, broad estimates of how the language policy are working out are all fine and desirable in themselves, but each parent and every child needs to feel assured that every single child in the school is under close review so far as his development is concerned. Success may or may not eventually be possible but the process of scrutinising and monitoring each child is. I think it very likely that this will, indeed, be standard in schools of the future, and because of the arguments I advanced earlier I have no doubt that such scrutiny ought to be the sole responsibility of the school and not of any outside agency. When schools fully accept this responsibility, they will have even more powerful claims than they have at present to resist those encroachments from outside which, I have tried to argue, can only have the effect of weakening the school's purpose and thus the quality of all the teaching and learning that go on there.

The parents' role

Schools are moving inevitably towards new relationships with parents. Evidence of change is, indeed, already to be seen on a wide scale. In my opinion, parents should have a powerful but strictly limited role. In brief, I do not believe that they should have any *power* over the curriculum or over the hiring, firing (and related matters) of staff. I do believe that *out of school* their role is one of such importance in the education of their children that it cannot be easily overstated. My discussion of early learning in Chapter 7 and of the acquisition of spoken language in Chapter 3 give, I believe, an account of this role, at least in outline. If one can ever claim that research has any conclusions, one can say that study after study has shown the importance of the parent (or, of course, of the surrogate parent) in the early years of a child's life. Moreover, the developmental analyses which I have been presenting throughout this book point in the same direction and emphasise the principle that learning has its foundations and that unless these are laid securely — and early — later learning is at peril.

And so there can be no doubt that parents have an obligation, among others, to extend the experiential basis of the child's learning. They need to talk to him even before he can himself talk. And, as he begins to understand language and to talk, they need to talk with him about his experiences, and to use language for a wide range of functions, including reminiscing and looking ahead in time. They need to use language that will explain, language that will excite, language that will intrigue. As they move in these directions, they will leave far behind the use of language merely to control and manage the child.

I feel strongly that this parental role should not be extinguished when the child begins school. Regular reading aloud and the discussion of books ought to continue. So ought taking the child to new and interesting places and talking about them. Such learning as then goes on is important in its own right, important in building the child's own self-regard and his feelings of competence and important in laying foundations and in buttressing what the school tries to do.

The question of whether parents should have a role inside school and away from curriculum decision-making is, perhaps, a harder one to answer. There are powerful reasons why they should have such a role, indeed, why they should have several roles, but there are also arguments against any close participation in the life of the school.

Some teachers feel very strongly that bringing parents into school, actively to further the children's education, is like mixing oil and water. Some of them hold that teaching children, especially in an institutional setting, is a professional matter, and that it ought to be the exclusive preserve of teachers. They may say this in order to avoid dilution or perhaps because they believe that the mysteries of the teaching craft are, for the most part, above the heads of the untrained. Others believe that parents in school are simply more trouble than they are worth. They may cramp the teacher's style and her methods of controlling the large numbers of children for whom she is responsible. Then there are matters of professional etiquette and propriety. For example, certain records are regarded as confidential and if they are not to be so regarded would often need to be recast. There might also be problems if parents were to take wrong or competitive attitudes to each other's children. Finding out that a particular child is 'backward' might give peculiar satisfactions to some of them. Besides, parents might discuss other people's children, particularly outside the proper setting in which a professional would engage in such discussions, and this would be regarded as distasteful or even as dangerous and disruptive.

These considerations all have force and some of them present considerable difficulties. However, many of them can be handled in such ways as considerably to reduce their dangers, and, in any case, the advantages of having parents in school on a regular and frequent basis seem vastly to outweigh them.

Earlier, I emphasised that parents need managing just as much as teachers do. Indeed, because of their lack of a relevant professional background, they need more managing. For instance, they need elementary training both in etiquette and in techniques. They need to be inducted into the ways of the school and to have explained to them the reasons why procedures are as they are. If they are asked to do any job, great or small, they should be carefully briefed so that they understand beyond doubt what is expected of them. They need to know where to operate, and what to do when they have finished their tasks. They may need help on how to deport themselves, on whether they may intervene in matters where they have not been invited to operate and how to judge whether what they are doing is successful. They may need constant reassurance and reiterated thanks. This brings us to an important principle. Parents coming in to school do not in any way detract from teachers' responsibilities: they add to them. To manage numbers of parents and to arrange it so that they play an important and useful part in the life of the school is a major management concern and must take up a significant part of the management resources that the Head and the staff can muster. Further, the need to review what parents do in school is no less acute than the need to review what teachers do — which, I have already argued, is supremely important. To keep whatever parents do under scrutiny is so important precisely because they are parents and not professionals. They do not have the years of training or that experience in dealing with numbers of children that mark out the teacher. They do not, that is, have comparable resources to fall back on. Further, there is always a chance that some parents may seek to exceed their proper function. They should know that they have an invaluable contribution to make, but that it is only as a member of a team that works in certain ways and according to certain procedures that they can have any role at all inside the school.

Given that such matters are constantly made clear and that parents can be used inside the school, what should they do? There is a range of functions but, on the whole, the object is not so much to replace the teacher as to amplify what she does. What follows is mainly directed to language work, but, of course, the point has been made that it is very difficult and often quite undesirable to separate language work from the rest of the curriculum Thus,

200

recruiting parents to help in such matters as preparing materials, for example by cutting paper or mixing paint, cleaning paint pots and brushes, catering for special occasions, superintending visits and escorting children to the baths or playing fields may not seem directly to be concerned with language work, but could nevertheless influence it informally or indirectly. More to the point are sessions where the parent is acting closer to the teaching role of the professional. Some parents, for example, conduct regular cooking sessions with children and the opportunities for language work here are immense — new vocabulary has to be acquired, new ways of giving directions have to be understood, new genres, such as recipes, have to be encountered, new ways of talking about new subjects to new adults have to be learned. Talking to children is also immensely important, though many parents will be bewildered unless they are told what they might talk about. Reading to children, especially if a parent can be induced to give a 'performance', is similarly enriching.

The schools of the near future will, I am convinced, be distinguished from schools of the past by their stance in relation to parents and the community. I am not thinking of what might seem to some to be encroachments on the proper spheres and responsibilities of teachers and would in the longer run paralyse or enervate them. Instead, I think parents will be seen as an extension of the human resources of the school which will permit schools to achieve far more than was ever possible in the past. At the same time schools will, I am equally sure, help and sustain parents in their own distinctive roles away from the school. Already, there are libraries of books and toy libraries from which parents may borrow. Mother and toddler clubs are part of the parent education movement. Parent-teacher associations often further extend this sort of work. On the whole, though, it is still in its infancy. As it develops, I hope that it will expand to take in not just mothers and fathers but also perhaps grandparents and other interested members of the community. Above all, I hope that when schools take on this family and community orientation it will always be with the clear aim of enhancing the education of children. There will be other beneficial results but there will be distortion unless education remains the clear focus of all that is done.

Select Bibliography

Ashworth, E. (1973) *Language in the junior school*, Edward Arnold, London

Barnes, D. (1976) *From communication to curriculum*, Penguin, Harmondsworth

Blank, D. (1973) *Teaching learning in the preschool: a developmental approach*, Merrill, Columbus, Ohio

Boden, M.A. (1979) *Piaget*, Fontana, London

Bruner, J.S. (1974) *Beyond the information given*, George Allen and Unwin, London

Chomsky, N. (1971) *Selected writings* (ed.) J.P.B. Allen and P. van Buren, Oxford University Press, London

Department of Education and Science (1975) *Primary education in England*, HMSO, London

Donaldson, M. (1978) *Children's minds*, Fontana/Collins, London

Gardner, K. *see* Lunzer, E. and Gardner, K.

Gruber, H.E. and Voneche, J.J. (1977) *The essential Piaget: an interpretive reference and guide*, Routledge and Kegan Paul, London

Halliday, M.A.K. (1973) *Explorations in the functions of language*, (includes 'Relevant models of language'), Edward Arnold, London

Hymes, Dell H. (ed.) (1964) *Language in culture and society: a reader in linguistics and anthropology*, Harper Row, New York

Kintsch, W. (1972) *Episodic and semantic memory* in Tulving, E. and Donaldson, W. (eds) *The organisation of memory*, Academic Press, New York

Kuhn, T. (1970) *The structure of scientific revolutions*, 2nd edn, Chicago University Press, Chicago

Lunzer, E. and Gardner, K. (1979) *The effective use of reading*, Heinemann, London

Lyons, J. (1970) *Chomsky*, Fontana/Collins, London

Moffett, J. (1968) *Teaching the universe of discourse*, Houghton Mifflin, Boston

Piaget, J. *see* Gruber, H.E. and Voneche, J.J. (eds)

Schaffer, H.R. (1977) *Mothering*, Fontana/Open Books, London

Tough, J. (1977) *Talking and learning*, Ward Lock Ed and Drake Ed. Ass., London

de Villiers, P.A. and J.G. (1979) *Early language*, Fontana/Open Books, London

Vygotsky, L.S. (1962) *Thought and language*, MIT Press, Cambridge, Mass.

Walkerdine, V. (1982) *From context to text: a psychosemiotic approach to abstract thought* in Beveridge, M. (ed.) *Children thinking through language*, Edward Arnold, London

Whorf, B.L. (1941) *The relation of habitual thought and behaviour to language* in Adams, P. *Language in thinking*, Penguin, Harmondsworth (1972)

Wells, G.S. (1981) *Learning through interaction*, Cambridge University Press, Cambridge

Index